NO MORE CHRISTIAN NICE GUY

Books by

Paul Coughlin

FROM BETHANY HOUSE PUBLISHERS

---

5 Secrets Great Dads Know

No More Christian Nice Girl (with Jennifer D. Degler)

No More Christian Nice Guy

No More Christian Nice Guy Study Guide

No More Jellyfish, Chickens, or Wimps

Unleashing Courageous Faith

Foreword by Dr. Laura Schlessinger

PAUL COUGHLIN

NO MORE

WHY BEING NICE—INSTEAD OF GOOD—

CHRISTIAN

HURTS MEN, WOMEN, AND CHILDREN

NICE GUY

BETHANYHOUSE
MINNEAPOLIS, MINNESOTA

Published by Bethany House Publishers
11400 Hampshire Avenue South
Bloomington, Minnesota 55438

Bethany House Publishers is a division of
Baker Publishing Group,
Grand Rapids, Michigan.

Printed in the United States of America

ISBN   978-0-7642-0369-5

Library of Congress has cataloged the hardcover edition as follows:

Coughlin, Paul T.
    No more Christian nice guy : when being nice—instead of good—hurts men, women, and children / Paul Coughlin ; foreword by Laura Schlessinger.
        p.   cm.
    Summary: "Christian nice guys believe in a 'gentle Jesus meek and mild.' Coughlin sets the record straight: a complete man who can be both gentle and bold is Jesus"—Provided by publisher.
    ISBN 0-7642-0092-5 (hardcover : alk. paper)
    1. Christian men—Religious life.   2. Men (Christian theology)   I. Title.
    BV4528.2.C67   2005
    248.8'42—dc22

                                                                    2005018447

To Sandy. For your support, encouragement, and more rejuvenation than you know.

To Elliot, Garrett, and Abigail "Wugs" Coughlin. You and Mom are at the core of this conspiracy of good.

AUTHOR BIO

PAUL COUGHLIN hosts a radio talk show in southern Oregon. He is the author of *No More Jellyfish, Chickens, or Wimps* and with his wife, Sandy, *Married . . . But Not Engaged.* Paul has been interviewed by C-SPAN, the *New York Times, Focus on the Family,* and numerous radio and television stations across the country. His articles have appeared in many publications, including *New Man, Faithworks,* and *Ministries Today.* He has also been editor of a weekly newspaper and a radio station program director. A former Christian Nice Guy, Paul is a happily married father of three. The Coughlin family lives in Oregon.

Christianniceguy.com

ACKNOWLEDGMENTS

When caught in a net not of your own making, it's difficult to identify everyone who was part of your captivity and freedom. Here are the major players.

A very special thank-you to Dr. Laura, Taffy Pelton Clarke, and Tom Coughlin Sr. Thank you, Dr. Kevin Leman, Janet Kobobel Grant, Ted Darnall, Tom Sabens, Stan Way, Robert Andrescik, Patrick Doyle, Bill Gallagher, Bob Just, Claire Widmark, Dan Buck, Daniel Weiss, Krista Carnet, Christopher Soderstrom, Jason Ehrlich, Kelly Wiebev, Rick Bundschuh, Steve Grensky, Brad Wilcox, Bob Albury, Mary Ellen Haynes, Tim Austin, Perry Atkinson, Senator Jason Atkinson, Jeff Smith, Michael Levine, and Cherie Snyder.

Thank you, D and J, mighty sources of blessed dissatisfaction.

TABLE OF CONTENTS

I n the last year I sold more than one million copies of *The Proper Care and Feeding of Husbands*. What makes this remarkable is that it wasn't a diet book, it didn't cover presidential red-blue politics, and it wasn't a thriller novel—and it definitely wasn't politically correct. This was a book focusing in on the rather standard mistreatment of men by their women and how a change in their attitude and behavior would virtually transform their men, their marriages, and their own lives into happier existences.

I expected a huge, ugly backlash. While I did get dismissive or harsh criticism from liberal, secular, feminist types, the general public—especially the men—was incredibly receptive. What touched me the most was the sad, pained, resigned letters I received from so many nice men who were suffering deeply. These men explained that while they were deeply in love with their wives, those wives were literally on a countdown: When the kids were all grown and gone, the men were going to leave as well. Why? Because they were abused and neglected. The abuse did not take the form of physical violence; it was the more subtle nagging, criticism, berating, demeaning, dismissing, and rejecting that has become commonplace in American marriages where men are looked upon as side dishes, not the main course.

The feminist movement, as well as the sexual revolution, continues to hurt women and men and their relationships. When Gloria Steinem enthusiastically proclaimed that "Women need men like fish need a bicycle," more than one generation of women was sent in the wrong direction in their search for love, security, bonding, and the joy of a quality marriage. Instead, women's organizations support behaviors that leave women alone and men designated as unimportant: unmarried sex as entertainment, shacking up without a commitment (marriage), single-mothering as a choice, abortions as birth control, no-fault divorce at will, men as oppressors or predators, and so forth. I often ask these women what they intend to say to their male children about their importance in this brave new female-oriented world. They don't have an answer.

Because we hardly raise men to be anything masculine anymore, we have at least two generations of men who have no clue what it means to be a "man." Hence, too many guys are, as I have lamented many times on my radio program, *males* instead of *men*.

Consequently, I get sad calls from women anguishing over the fact that their husbands demand they abandon the children to day care to bring in more money. I am amazed how different this is from fifty years ago, when a man would fall on his sword before he would expect that. Today's males have had their innate urge to provide and protect removed from their spines, guts, heads, hearts, and souls.

I also get calls from women who complain that their guy has had sex with them, shacked up with them, made babies with them, and then moved on to other conquests. The whole blame, in their minds, is on the men! Unbelievable! When I bring to their attention that for every step of the way (unmarried sex, all birth control has risk, living together without marriage, no spiritual center to their relationships) they were complicit, they get angry with me. It seems that women have been trained to have "no rules" but still blame men when things don't go as their fantasies would lead them.

Feminists always excuse the horrendous behavior of women (Andrea Yates and Susan Smith, for example) as a product of their oppression in society as a woman, wife, and mother, but condemn men for the same crimes as "evil." Feminists always excuse the irresponsible behavior of women (welfare, out-of-wedlock multiple-fathered children) as a product of their limited opportunities and power in a patriarchal society, but condemn men for the same behaviors (a huge percentage of our sports heroes) as bums and users.

The bottom line is that men are blamed for their own and women's misbehaviors. Somehow, that doesn't seem to be the mentality you'd expect from groups that espouse "empowering" women.

I have been on the radio, taking calls from men and women, for about thirty years. I have seen many trends. I can tell when "something's happening" by virtue of the pressure of a type of question or caller. It is clear to me that there isn't a consensus on what "being a man" means. Women give mixed, confused signals and messages because women are basically confused between what they're being indoctrinated to want and what they really want. Clint Eastwood, Keanu Reeves, Kevin Costner, Russell Crowe, Denzel Washington, and others are examples of strong, primal animal men. Women are drawn to such strength (epitomized by the high-school bad boys) because, biologically, women are drawn to men who can provide and protect so that they can be safe raising their babies. Russell Crowe's character in *Gladiator* was especially enthralling to women because he had great abs, fighting strength, intense will, and he wouldn't have sex with an available, attractive woman because he was being true to his murdered wife.

Men today are being influenced to be "metrosexual," which is, in my opinion, just another term for emasculated; men are to be women with different genitals. This is not good for them, for women, for society, for democracy, for families.

I frankly can't believe how many men call me with problems in their families that they feel impotent to deal with, exert any authority, or take any stand. Some women might imagine they like being the only power in their home lives (if that's so, marry a momma's boy whose momma is deceased); most women realize the blessing that a healthy partnership brings. I can't tell you how many times I've had to remind men that they are *men,* and that this designation is not about biology; it is about strength, will, honor, courage, leadership, sacrifice, compassion, and love.

Here I am, a nice Jewish mother, writing the foreword for a book about Christian Nice Guys. Why? Because, within the context of Christian Scripture, there is a message for all of us: Men and women are created differently, equal in value, but different. The unisex, anti-male mentality that has infiltrated all our institutions, even our religious ones, has not brought cooperation, love, and serenity to our homes and lives. In order for our children to become happy, functional, loving, contributing members of this world, they need the support and structure that an intact, happy home can bring. I see *No More Christian Nice Guy* as a step in that direction.

—Dr. Laura Schlessinger

Author, *The Proper Care and Feeding of Husbands*

CHRISTIAN NICE GUYS AREN'T SO NICE

You must accept that fear is not only harmful but evil, not only unhelpful but deeply destructive.

— R A B B I   S H M U L E Y   B O T E A C H

The ordinary man is passive. . . . Against major events he is as helpless as against the elements. So far from endeavoring to influence the future, he simply lies down and lets things happen to him.

— G E O R G E   O R W E L L

What do you think would happen if Jesus were to appear at your church next Sunday and say to people what he says in the Bible?

"Hypocrites!"

"White-washed tombs."

"Fools!"

"Dull."

And "a brood of vipers fit for hell!"

Given how *nice* the church expects Christian men to be, I think we'd rush the pulpit and wrest the microphone from his hand. "*Tsk, tsk, tsk,*" we'd mutter scornfully. We'd wag our fingers, reminding him of the supreme importance placed on manners and appearances in this holy place.

Some women, reaching for soap bars to wash out his mouth, would recite our unofficial church motto: "If you don't have anything nice to say, Jesus, don't say it at all." *He really should be ashamed of himself.*

Shame is big in the church. Helps keep guys in line. Keeps their heads down. Keeps them humble. Supposedly.

Actually, without shame, guys might be able to live the vital life God intended. This world would be a lot better.

Instead, we have *passive, naïve Christian Nice Guys.* We sit next to them in church all the time, not realizing their identity is being squashed, their will being broken, the lives of those who love and depend upon them being diminished as well. Everyone loses when we follow a false ideal.

That Christian men are expected to follow a nonexistent Jesus hinders and frustrates those of us who possess a vital masculine nature but are told not to activate it. I say throw the switch and don't apologize—you'll be more like the real Christ when you do. I pray that this book will show you how.

Not so long ago I would have joined this mob—er, crowd—shushing Jesus. That's because I believed in a Savior who doesn't really exist. Many of us believe in a wooden Jesus who was perpetually somber, consistently robotic, consummately nice. He wouldn't *think* of hurling sarcasm at anyone; his momma raised a Nice Boy with impeccable manners. Many sermons we hear are designed to make Jesus appear *always* approachable, *always* calm, and *endlessly* patient. That's fiction right up there with *The Da Vinci Code;* this mild Jesus has more to do with Eastern mysticism than with the gospel record. He did *not* remain "above it all," emotionally hovering above us silly little humans. He got down in the muck and mire of life with us. He really lived; he really felt eye-watering joy and soul-crushing pain. He didn't assume the Lotus, drinking tea and finding us mildly amusing while trying to clear his head of conflict and division. Jesus, the dissident, brought the world both—the kind of conflict and division needed to shake things up for our own good.

JESUS, SUPREME NICE GUY

When we reach those sticky parts of the New Testament where Jesus lost his cool and called people names, we still portray him as having a gleam in his eye or as suppressing a kind smile, because Jesus would never be *that* rude. He wasn't really mad, says the underlying message. He just raised his voice a little to get everyone's attention, like a tour guide on a busy street.

I once treated exclamation points that followed expressions such as "hypocrites!" and "brood of vipers fit for hell!" as if they were merely biblical italics. Jesus was *emphasizing* a point—He didn't actually yell at anyone. . . . Talk about spin. I did a lot of damage control for my Savior.

I created my own sanitized, unauthorized translation, *The Nice Guy Bible* (NGB), which I continue to see a lot of other guys carrying around. I rewrote some parts and took others out of context to hide from God and from what he really wanted of me. I kept this distortion of Jesus neatly in my mind, the way a Nice Guy feels he should, until it was destroyed by an unusual and unexpected epiphany: Christ's humor. His blessed sarcasm helped me begin to see how he *actually* lived and talked, as opposed to how I'd thought. A mental fog lifted. At last my life received a long-needed clarity. I neared the red-hot bonfire of truth, which warmed and saved me. A greater taste for life awakened.

> **I created my own sanitized, unauthorized translation, *The Nice Guy Bible* (NGB), which I continue to see a lot of other guys carrying around.**

I began to ask questions like: How come when we ask, WWJD? we almost always assume some form of quiet, mellow response, when he often spoke and behaved in undeniably rugged ways? If Jesus said we are to be wise as serpents and innocent as doves, why have I heard countless sermons admonishing me to live in innocence—a more gentle virtue—but precious few on how to apply wisdom, a more rough-and-tumble virtue that sometimes requires conflict?

Looking back, I once believed this caricature of "gentle Jesus, meek and mild" because it was what I internalized during well-orchestrated church services designed to make God palatable to contemporary taste buds. I was told, though not in so many words, that the safe and pleasant route is really the best.

The popular fiction that Jesus is the Supreme Nice Guy no longer holds any water for me. Have you seen the bumper sticker that reads "Jesus Is My Best Friend"? Puh-leese. I don't ask my best friends to forgive me for my sins. I don't pray to my best friends. I don't worship my best friends. The Lamb of God is also the Lion of Judah. He is *good*, but I can't say he is *nice*.

It gets worse. Christian Nice Guys (CNGs) are even told that by turning themselves into involuntary doormats for others (something they often mistake for sacrificial giving), they will somehow, magically, against all understanding of human nature and experience, lead others to Christ. Is this really WJWD? Do people really regard a world view as true because its followers are nice, easy, and possess smooth etiquette?

Bill Hybels says that passive Christians repel non-Christians from the faith:

> I've learned through the years that seekers are not impressed with spinelessness. . . . Most of the time, seekers . . . respect and admire Christians who aren't afraid to take a stand. . . .
>
> Let me say it once more: Seekers have little respect for weak Christians. Deep down they're looking for somebody—anybody—to step up and proclaim the truth and then to live it boldly. (*Becoming a Contagious Christian*, 63–64.)

HEARING WHAT WE WANT TO HEAR

Not that the church bears all the blame. It would be so much simpler and so much less embarrassing if it did. *I heard what I wanted to hear.* And I believed in this misrepresentation of my Lord because, like millions of other Christian Nice Guys, I couldn't handle the truth (or didn't believe I could). I couldn't fully experience his love because of the degree to which fear controlled me. When fear and its evil buddy anxiety are in the driver's seat, forget the incomparable abundance and freedom Jesus offers but also warns is hard to find.

As someone who was conditioned to always be pleasant, not to bother others, and, for the wrong reasons, be quick to turn the cheek, I held the classic distorted Nice Guy view of myself. I believed I was defective and bad, not because of my sin, but because my perception was off. *Others* were worthy of respect if for no other reason than to have their human dignity affirmed. *Me?* Well, do what you want to me, because I—my thoughts, my feelings, my wants, my needs—don't really matter. *Other* people were normal; *I* was a sort of subspecies, a child of a lesser god. This, as I explain later, kept me from God's love and from truly loving others. The Jesus I heard about was always brokenhearted over my sin, which I kept making him pay for. He was worn out, tormented, aloof; a drained, pale man frozen in the iceberg of history's tragedy—he looked as if he needed saving too. And his Father was angry and sorely disappointed with me, Mr. Screw-Up.

This script, this understanding of God, ensured that my life would remain tiny, unnoticeable, and worse, innocuous. Moreover, if I could hide all this behind the guise of "Christian humility," all the better!

The demeaning and undercutting screenplay owned my mind like a commercial slogan, a message I learned as a kid. (A kid who went through some tough times, which I'll share with you in chapter 4.) You might perceive that the sorrow I experienced is more or less than yours, but I don't believe pain is quantifiable, and degree of difficulty isn't the main issue. It's the result that counts, and it's the result that keeps CNGs down.

The convincing, repetitive message of my inherent worthlessness helped lay waste to my life in disastrous ways, stealing my passion, energy, and resources, and churning my gut, which is where resentment and anxiety live. My name is Paul, and I'm a former Christian Nice Guy who finally realized that what we call valorous niceness is often cowardly passivity in disguise.

THE MELLOW-YELLOW WORLD OF CHRISTIAN NICE GUYS

CNGs pretty much believe they should just let life happen to them. A large portion of the church tells them they should rarely if ever exert their will, that possessing passion, boldness, and intensity is wrong and "worldly." *Those* qualities belong to "aggressive" and "proud" men. (Ironically, including Jesus.) Many have told me that it's far more Christian to live limply, deny your heart's desires, and keep your life in neutral because somehow, brother, this glorifies God.

The church told me to worry more about sin than purpose, more about keeping up appearances than searching for and embracing meaning. More about what I shouldn't do than what I should do. More about being nice than being good. Fear of failure, of falling short, of trying, but not being perfect, has us paralyzed, immobile, and, eventually, indifferent.

Fear-based religiosity creates dangerous tension that ruins marriages, careers, children—sometimes even our souls. We *should* avoid sin, for many reasons—that it separates us from God and from life are atop my list. *But so does the immobile life. It's just harder to diagnose.*

Think about how pleasing the illusion of a conflict-free life is to the ears of Nice Guys. Who can confront them with criticism if they don't do anything noticeable? No one goes through the embarrassment of getting a speeding ticket when inside a parked car.

Another who has noted the perplexing prevalence of Christian male passivity is theologian R. C. Sproul, who says,

> When I became a Christian, I understood that Jesus took my sin away. What I never heard from Him was that He intended to take my backbone away.

Nice Guys don't think they should stand up for themselves and for others. The church widely teaches that good Christians don't do conflict . . . and CNGs rejoice in the widespread acceptance of this anti-biblical message, because conflict is their kryptonite. Contrary to fine-tuned façades, this avoidance has little to do with the virtue of being kind. It has everything to do with the vice of fearful passivity.

Whether explicitly or tacitly, visibly or covertly, fear cripples Christian Nice Guys, until they face it with honesty and integrity. Then, in stunning reversal, these fears behave like the demons that possessed the man Jesus healed: They ask for permission to inhabit pigs instead, because *they* can't handle the confrontation, and it's a kick to watch them scamper. But there's that dreaded word again, *confront.* I want to show you how to confront this fear, the schoolyard bully that haunts CNGs into adulthood. Like all such bullies, it's weak. All bluff. Fear can't handle God's truth about you.

Think about it, Nice Guys: Wouldn't it be great to view conflict as an event you could enter into with moderation, tact, and wisdom, the way you've seen other men embrace it? To be freed from the shackles of niceness, a fearful vice that takes on the deceptive posture of virtue, an idol that distances you from God and from others? Marriages would be saved, our culture war would gain new and powerful members, children would get a dad to admire, missions would be launched, and God's redemptive plan would transform yet another dark realm of this messed-up world.

Maybe it's killing you right now. You're thinking, *What's wrong with being nice?!*

That all depends on what we mean when we use this deceptively adaptable term. Think about the "nice" people in your life, then ask yourself, for instance: Do they stand up to injustice? Do they fight against what they know to be untrue?

No. They don't have it in them. "Nice" can't confront this world's sources of pain, the way Jesus did and commanded us to do as well. Niceness makes people agreeable, not good.

> **"Nice" can't confront this world's sources of pain. Niceness makes people agreeable, not good. Somehow we have mistaken niceness for righteousness.**

Somehow we have mistaken niceness for righteousness, when the Bible says that the righteous are as bold as lions. Good grief, nice people are anything but bold—many just hide in timid politeness behind misleading smiles. I once did.

Though they often are pleasant to be around, the nice often hide from life's unpleasant and disturbing messiness. They often conceal that they do not possess a redemptive power behind their veneer of pleasantness. Their fear and inaction brings suffering to them and to those around them.

The meaning of the word *nice* is as unreliable as the people it describes. Today it is synonymous with "pleasant" and "agreeable," but it has also meant "effeminate," "unmanly," "unable to endure much," "dainty," "reluctant," "ignorant," and "difficult to please." Nevertheless, remarkably, Christian men can be shunned in church and home if they are not unfailingly pleasant, agreeable, and in possession of impeccable manners. These attributes of niceness are taken to be expressions of a Spirit-filled life, yet none of these words or concepts are biblically mentioned as part of the Spirit's fruit.

Besides, the mind of a Christian Nice Guy is anything but pleasant or agreeable. For reasons explained later, these men are often secretive and manipulative. They harbor hissing resentments, and, given all the games they feel they need to play just to survive, their wives (*if* they can hold on to a wife) may come to question their own sanity. Though they inwardly exhaust themselves in their determination to hide it, they are easily irritated and frustrated. When nasty behavior surfaces, they may mistakenly or dismissively explain it away as the result of testosterone fluctuation or workplace preoccupation. They may label it a kind of male menopause, which is the trend today, or give it a name like Irritable Male Syndrome, which largely ignores a profound spiritual component.

Appearances are deceiving, as this wife of a CNG laments:

> Before we were married, he did all types of things to prove he handled issues. Two weeks after the wedding, off came the gloves. And he told me under no circumstances am I to open my mouth. I barely made it through the first year. I have struggled to stay married to him. . . .

His attitudes, mood swings, explosive screaming fits, all the things he has held in, all come out. . . . My husband tells me all the time he is just a Nice Guy. He isn't, and he isn't nice to be married to, either.

Not every CNG is *that* abusive and phony. As with every condition that hinders abundant living, the Christian Nice Guy problem shows itself by degrees. Here's a self-test to help you discover if it's gumming up your life. If you answer yes to one or two, the nice guy problem is in your blood and it may well get worse. Yes to three to five, and you're a runaway train of destruction—with a deceptive smiley face on the locomotive. Stop what you're doing, clear out your schedule, and get busy with your life. If you have a husband, boyfriend, son, or grandson who you suspect is a CNG, take this test for them and go with what your gut tells you. Try not to overanalyze each question. Usually the first answer that pops into your mind is the accurate one. Don't show him the result. Just keep reading. You'll get a detailed road map of where to go from here.

FAITH LIFE

- Do you dismiss or never discuss parts of the Bible where Jesus isn't nice?
- When wondering "WWJD," do you assume a gentle response?
- Do you think conflict and anger are sins?
- Are you the guy at church who never says no to an assignment, even if it diminishes other important aspects of your life?
- Do you think that being nice, observing etiquette, and knowingly allowing yourself to be used by others nevertheless leads people to salvation?

HOME LIFE

- Are you attracted to or married to a woman who needs to be rescued? Do you think of her as "a diamond in the rough"?

○ Do you lack leadership in your family?

○ Do you make your wife the emotional center of your life?

○ Are you unclear with your wife about your sexual desires?

○ Do you often settle for unfulfilling sex?

WORK LIFE

○ Do you find yourself saying one thing to one person but something different to another?

○ Do you smile even when you don't like what's happening to you, then rant or fume about it later?

○ Do you hide your mistakes, even when the consequences are little or none?

○ Do you find yourself working for abusive bosses?

○ Do you make less money than you know you should?

LIFE IN GENERAL

○ Do you feel embarrassed when people compliment you?

○ Are you envious when you see other men showing deep emotion?

○ Do women like talking with you, but then show no romantic interest?

○ Do you think it's selfish to have your own wants and desires?

○ Do you think avoiding conflict will make your life better?

○ If someone is angry with you, do you automatically believe or sense that they're right to feel that way?

○ Do you hide your flaws, even from those close to you?

○ Does fear often stop you from moving ahead?

○ Do you think being nice will make you stand out among other men?

PROFILES OF THE CHRISTIAN NICE GUY

Place yourself in the two-faced world of a Christian Nice Guy: On the surface you appear happy, pleasant, and seem to exude humility and meekness. You turn your cheek to most every injury, insult, and injustice, not because you are following Christ's command (though that's what you tell yourself and others), but because you unilaterally fear conflict. You are nice not because you are virtuous, but because you lack virtue. And during those rare moments where you do protect yourself or others, it's usually overblown and causes needless pain for everybody. (Hence the famous term *passive-aggressive*.) You lack the ability to speak the truth in love, which is fundamental to both a fruitful and assertive personality, the very kind of personality you desperately want, but can't seem to obtain.

Outside, and especially at church, you're warm and friendly; you appear to care about others. Inside, however, you may carry frustration and rage, because you are doubly haunted: You get to experience the weight and consequence of your own sin (much of which you try to hide through timid lies) *and* the weight and consequence of believing that you are inferior to your fellowman and that you lack intrinsic worth as a human being made in God's image. Refer to all this as psychobabble if you want (I once did), but realize you might do so at your own peril. The Bible clearly tells us how to approach this: We are to "encourage the timid, help the weak" (1 Thessalonians 5:14).

Do you manipulate others in creative ways? Do you especially control your wife and children, who then suffer in silence? Do you cover your fear with behavior that appears exceptional and praiseworthy? Does your inner angst come out suddenly and sideways? Does it anger you that others seem to have unquestionable power in your life, while you feel helpless? When your wife is sexually unavailable, do you get back at her with sexual fantasies that include other (known or nameless) women? Do you steal from your boss as a way of retaliating for his mistreatment of you?

Hopefully at some point, your cover's blown. Because I've seen the process firsthand, I want your life to be deconstructed, and I want the Nice Guy fallacy to be acknowledged as the sham it is. If you take ownership of your life and the issues that keep you passive, then what you may call a catastrophe is likely the beginning of a better life for you and for those who love you. You don't need to walk around with a scarlet *P* on your forehead; you *will* need a willingness to try something different that will lead to something better.

Later I'll explain how to escape the lifestyle that diminishes CNGs. Honesty and integrity will flourish in ways you always wanted but couldn't enact. An unfamiliar power will flow once your "disease to please" is gone. Confidence, always so elusive, will replace crippling fear. Dreams will be dusted off and bolstered by newfound shrewdness, wisdom, and the good kind of cunning—three qualities Jesus exercised and said we should also. Purpose will finally enliven your days and bless your sleep. Hope will grow, and with it a daring belief that God, who deep inside you thought was your greatest critic, is really your supreme advocate. Your better life will become a living testimony to his redemptive power and grace.

For Christian Nice Guys that presently feel surrounded by foes, this new reality will erase many dilemmas, phobias, and accusations, inner demons that collectively form a circular barbed-wire fence with no apparent gate. When a man perceives himself to be trapped inside, those immediately outside—those wanting and needing his love, his affirmation, his protection, his provision—are left confused and disillusioned. Sons are hit between the eyes, struggling with what it means to be a man, because in our earnest attempts to make them kinder, we've made them softer.

Wives, girlfriends, and daughters are among the hardest hit. When I talk about this powerful topic, they shake my hand, sometimes even grab my elbow at the same time. They look deep into my (stranger) eyes and say with a heavy heart, "You just described my husband . . . boyfriend . . . father." They don't condemn their men; their basic goodwill toward them is still intact, but their Nice Guy has yet to chew through it. "What can I do?" they ask me.

A wife asks why her Christian husband won't stand up to defend and protect their family; she also doesn't understand why he's always nice to others, yet secretly so cruel to her.

Friends don't know why their Christian buddy won't walk alongside them and make himself available during difficult times.

A worried mother asks why her son won't speak up for himself, even though it's ruining his senior year in high school.

A grandmother tells of being tired of seeing men portrayed as worthless fools in the media. She knows her grandsons are watching, marinating in this shame-producing poison, and she worries for their souls.

A boss wonders why his Christian employee won't get his department into shape, even after many meetings and warnings.

Children are confused as to why their Christian father appears to be such a strong and stable presence at church—always smiling and nodding—but then seems to physically and emotionally abandon them when they most obviously need protection and affection.

> **Children are confused as to why their Christian father appears to be such a strong and stable presence at church—always smiling and nodding—but then seems to physically and emotionally abandon them when they most obviously need protection and affection.**

A woman likes her Christian boyfriend, but can't deny the lack of some necessary spark. She feels horrible, perhaps even ashamed that it's not there; wonders if there's something wrong with her, not him. She practices in her mind those dreaded words to say and hear: "Can't we just be friends?" Or "You have a great personality, but . . ." The CNG thinks to himself, *Dogs have personalities too.* He secretly loathes that this always happens to him, and he blames God (though he tries to be nice about it). *How come Nice Guys don't get the girl?* he asks himself in smoldering resentment (while still forcing his painted-on smile).

A pastor scratches his head and wonders why some of the men in his church just can't "get their act together."

The chair of a state political party is mystified as to why Christian men rigidly avoid social and civic activity.

Some of these puzzles once shrouded my life as well, so please know there are no stones in my hands. Just empathy and some sound guidance that I'm excited to share with you.

What you're about to read is a before-and-after story, an intimate slice of the Christian Nice Guy phenomenon, which by now is chewing through yet another generation of troubled males. I was once a CNG, who had a Damascus Road–like experience with Christ's real, rugged righteousness. I'm not that same man anymore.

A path toward freedom awaits you, a path that begins with an explanation of where the damage began. This will show how passive Nice Guys are made, not born. The initial good news: *If you're a Nice Guy, that's not the real you.* There's something and someone stronger and better inside you that's waiting to be vitalized and released; the true you, the "you" God created, *can* thrive.

> **We choke on a Victorian Jesus, a caricature that has turned men into mice.**

We'll take a look at what an earnest but troubling message from the church has done to men, creating an unintentional side effect that we battle today: We choke on a Victorian Jesus, a caricature that has turned men into mice.

We'll also examine the problems handed to men by our culture, a culture that at best is confused about genuine masculinity and at worst vilifies it. We'll see how Nice Guys lie to themselves and to the world around them, making matters worse for everyone. I'll explain how these streams of influence converge to drown a CNG at home, church, and work. Combining all facets of the conundrum is overwhelming; fortunately we don't serve a soft Savior, and God has not destined us to be eternal Nice Guys.

This book is part inspirational (a category of books I used to ridicule), part instructional, and part manifesto. I'm a guy who has sat through more than twenty-five years of church and who has been tempted to leave in response to its misdirected disregard of men—of manhood—and the unnecessary suffering it has caused.

(I know many who *have* left; their testimonies are on these pages. They're angry with their culture, their church, and their God, and sometimes their anger is directed at women. Nowhere in this book will you find a validation of abuse or any justification to mistreat another person. We'll focus on refining such anger, retaining its energy and passion, so it can be transformed into a redemptive force.)

I decided that instead of the passive-aggressive route, I would take action. This is the fruit of my labor, my personal Wittenberg Door. Like Martin Luther, here I stand—I can do no other, because I can hold my tongue no longer. Like many men, I have felt needlessly but undeniably out of place in the church, so I'm creating a place of truth and strength for myself and other men who love God, but who've had it with being shamed for being men.

And I'm not leaving either. I'm in it for the long haul, because like my Savior, I love a good fight. It's time to put on our boots. It's time for the Good Guy Rebellion.

I call this a rebellion because the church, for all its goodness and beauty, is not going to give men permission to completely embrace their masculinity and all of its traits. No wonder women outnumber men in every form of Christianity (with the possible exception of Eastern Orthodoxy). Outrageously, we mistake women's better attendance as proof that they are somehow more moral and spiritual, a false conclusion from flawed premises.

What you're about to read is on the edge—some will say over the edge—of what most of us have called "Christian living." Not everyone will agree with my conclusions. I ask for your charity and for suspension of judgment till the end of the book; for now, allow me to seek the fix for a problem that in one form or another plagues every Christian man and many non-Christians as well. On this I think we'll all agree: The center of our lives isn't holding, and it hasn't for a long time. It's time for a new approach, though it isn't really new: It's been hiding in plain view for nearly two thousand years.

CHAPTER

JESUS THE BEARDED WOMAN

There has got abroad a notion, somehow, that if you become a Christian you must sink your manliness and turn milksop.

— C . H . S P U R G E O N

[We have] efficiently pared the claws of the Lion of Judah, certified Him as a fitting household pet for pale curates and pious old ladies.

— D O R O T H Y S A Y E R S

"He is out of his mind."

— J E S U S ' F A M I L Y , W H O T R I E D T O S E I Z E H I M (M A R K 3 : 2 1)

Christian men across denominational divides are told to follow an example of right behavior that doesn't exist. They are told to behave "like Jesus," but are shown an incomplete portrait that fortifies their passivity. We need to see and emulate *all* of Jesus, gentle and rugged and all points in between. This means we'll have to push past prejudices and fears, for the record is clear: Jesus traveled the entire tender/tough spectrum without apology, and he says we must emulate him, so the real rub is elsewhere. Frequently we don't want to accept this because we think its ramifications are too demanding; what we fail to see, what I failed to see, is that *not* traveling the entire spectrum of life is far more demanding. While following God is hard sometimes, nothing, ultimately, is harder than not following him.

BOWING TO A FALSE IMAGE

Another who has noticed this inaccurate portrayal of Christ is Stu Weber, author of *The Heart of a Tender Warrior,* in which he laments,

> **While following God is hard sometimes, nothing, ultimately, is harder than not following him.**

> Why is it when someone says, "Picture the archetypal male," the image that comes to mind is not one of Jesus? I have to confess that, for years, the picture in my mind would not have been Jesus. Even the single most famous portrait of Jesus makes Him look more like a pouting model for Breck shampoo than a man.

Rick Bundschuh, author of *Passed Thru Fire: A Call for a Christian Rite of Passage to Guide Boys Into Godly Manhood,* writes about a picture of Jesus his family was given, noting that it accurately represents the view of our Savior given many of us from the church:

> Jesus was a gaunt, pasty white creature hidden under mounds of flowing robes. . . . His hair was long, thin, and stringy. He was painted to look strained, tired and supplicant. Gentle Jesus, meek and mild. Soft and suspiciously effeminate. It often seems as if the church is working in collusion with a culture bent on emasculating men and turning raw male material into pliable, defanged images of its own liking.

Frederica Mathewes-Green said this after seeing a mall display of the manger scene:

> [It was] plump with stupidity. Jesus as a cookie. God as a pet. This is very bad news. For one thing, a circle of cuddly bears is useless at helping us deal with pain. It cannot help us grasp searing heartbreak. . . .

> We want a just-my-size God, fluffy and approachable, without all
> those picky commandments. But once we get him down to teddy-bear
> size we find that he is powerless. He is not able to ease our suffering
> or comprehend our dark confusions; he does not have strength equal
> to our grief. A reduced God is no God at all. (*God As Suffering Parent*)

A reduced God is what popular author Phillip Yancey once upheld. The real Jesus, he writes, is far less tame than the one he found in Bible college:

> In my prior image, I realized, Jesus' personality matched that of a
> *Star Trek* Vulcan: he remained calm, cool, and collected as he strode
> like a robot among excitable human beings on spaceship earth. That
> is not what I [later] found portrayed in the Gospels. . . . Indeed, he
> seemed more emotional and spontaneous than the average person,
> not less. More passionate, not less. (*The Jesus I Never Knew*)

Still, the false image prevails. We need to know why. Then the fun part—we get to blow it up.

UNCHAINED SON

It's hell being a Christian Nice Guy until you embrace Christ's tough, courageous, protective, assertive personality, which invigorates real male sensibilities. These qualities are found on the more rugged end of the male spectrum, currently not well represented in the church, which overemphasizes Christ's gentler side at the expense of honest and healthy balance.

Here's a story that I hope will help to clarify. I call it the Parable of Jim.

Jim is a thirty-something teacher to whom people are drawn. But Jim breaks all kinds of rules. He's confrontational, opinionated, filled with willpower.

He threatens to fight scoundrels who are making money off of religion, even grabbing their TV camera, a tool for this sordid gain, and smashing it to the ground, creating one long commercial break.

He has called his students dumb and dull, asking how much longer he'll have to endure their company.

In order to stem his influence, his enemies play word games and devise interview scenarios in which to embarrass him; he's so cunning and shrewd that he constantly shows them up instead. No one has the guts to talk the way he does. Others talk like they understand God; Jim talks like he knows God. Jim forcefully disrupts the order of things and disregards convention. Jim's inappropriate.

He calls people bad names that "respectable men" never say. He verbally confronts one of his most powerful government officials. When Jim has faced an authority figure who, because of manufactured charges, could actually invoke the death penalty, Jim's slow-to-come responses have been obscure, searing, and disrespectful.

Jim doesn't mind his manners around important persons. Jim causes problems for society's respectable people. No wonder they want to pull him down.

In one public speech, to illustrate a profound spiritual truth, Jim has spoken of excrement going into a drain. He's colorful, but some think his language is too coarse for a spiritual leader, and the press has a field day: *PREACHER OR POTTYMOUTH? YOU DECIDE.*

He has told reporters that his mission isn't to discover or promote a lifetime of warm and cozy. *Au contraire:* "I bring division and conflict! Live as I say you should," he tells morning news shows over coffee and crumpets, and it may "tear your families apart!" Then he states the obvious: "Those who don't find me offensive will be blessed." *Who booked this guy?* Regis wonders, glancing at security, hoping they're keeping a sharp eye. *Who in the world does he think he is?* muse countless others.

Jim is sarcastic, sometimes bitingly so; he doesn't apologize. Jim goes to parties *and* hangs out with others who do. At least once he has supplied the wine, for free, during a wedding where children were likely present. Drinks are on him, even though he knows he'll be accused of corrupting others and touting sinfulness. The bureaucrats and government workers with whom he spends time are the ones everybody else hates. Jim doesn't even shun mentally imbalanced devotees or politically leprous radicals.

Many murmur and complain that they don't understand him. His own students sometimes won't ask him questions because they fear his response.

Most religious leaders enjoy the attention of large crowds, but Jim's wary: He doesn't trust them, and he doesn't hide his distrust. He actually confronts empty compliments during public gatherings—not a seeker-friendly ministry approach. Even though he still takes students, Jim's been unemployed for at least three years and doesn't even look for a job. He lives off handouts, owns no property, doesn't even have his own cardboard box to return to at night.

If we compare these actions of Jesus to the behavior expected of the average guy in most churches today—and, if we were honest—we'd say, absurdly, that *Christ is not a "Christian."* We wouldn't pray to him; we'd issue prayer requests *for* him.

One choice that led to further attacks was Jim's allowing a prostitute—in public—to anoint him with rare and expensive oil that could have been used to feed the poor, support missionaries, or pay for part of a child's life-saving surgery. While his students *and* his opponents boiled with anger over this wasteful extravagance, Jim would not hear it denounced and had the audacity to say that whenever God's liberating message is preached, this one event will be mentioned favorably. The woman wiped Jim's feet with her own hair, a lure she has used to draw men to her bed, but he has no care for his reputation. The scandal of it all! Hear the good folk gossip! Film at eleven!

He warns his students that people will despise them. Some will even be brought to court by blackmailers with unfair charges. Jim tells them to pay off the blackmailer before it goes that far. He instructs one student to sell some clothing in order to buy a weapon.

Jim, who's loving, kind, and compassionate, is not owned or influenced by fear and shame. Still, he does all the above and more, which begs the question: Do you think Jim's a "good Christian man"? Is he a Nice Guy?

This *is* part of the life of Christ as recorded in the Gospels, but are you surprised by how foreign some of it looks? If we compare these actions of Jesus to the behavior expected of the average guy in most churches today—

and, if we were honest—we'd say, absurdly, that *Christ is not a "Christian."* We wouldn't pray to him; we'd issue prayer requests *for* him.

Something doesn't add up.

I hope you are beginning to see how some men are isolated from the church not because they are "backsliders" but because of what they're told they must be in order to find peace and contentment. There *are* men to whom following Jesus means abandoning these common misconceptions about him. I know these men. They believe they have no choice. They have asked, as I have, if Jesus is pleased with how we, the church, presently portray him; they can't honestly say yes.

I constructed "Jim's story" to help us get past our extreme caricature of the Nice Nazarene. By now some well-read domesticated bird is staring down at the Parable of Jim, reading upside down and wondering why it's lining his cage. So be it. But for those who haven't yet torn up all or part of this book, realize that *this characterization is concentrated toughness,* and just as you don't want to consume a sludge of orange juice concentrate, neither do you want to run off with *this* caricature of Jesus: It's the other extreme, the inverse swing of the pendulum from our current banal portrayal of Jesus the Bearded Woman.

A WHOLE OTHER GOSPEL

It's a whole other gospel when your Nice Guy glasses are thrown in the garbage. Mark records more of Christ's rugged side than any other account, and with Mark at the wheel, you're in the passenger seat, white-knuckled, reminding yourself to breathe. There is no seat belt, and as Mark goes off road, you rejoice to realize that being nice isn't the point of Christianity.

Here are some of the words and phrases in just the first chapter of Mark that describe the world in which Jesus warred: shouting, wilderness, sins, camel hair, locusts, slave, split open, tempted, Satan, arrested, the time has come!, possessed, evil spirit, destroy, be quiet!, screamed, convulsed, amazement, high fever, victims, alone, leprosy, begging, moved with pity, be healed!, examine, secluded. And, according to the oldest and best manuscripts, Mark's gospel ends (in 16:8) with a word we all dread: *afraid.*

None of this is comfortable or pleasant. None of us, when under the spell of the fake virtue called niceness, says a loud "Amen" to this roughness. But wait till the hazy ethereal spell is broken: You'll hunger and thirst for more as the Good News takes on lungs, meat, and sinew. The gospel includes dirty feet, stinky hair, fish guts, bugs between its teeth, dirt under its nails—it's entrenched in life's day-to-day. Smell the adrenaline, feel your heart pound, taste the locust that lingers on your lips. God is on the loose. Hunting us down! Warring to liberate us from anything and everything that seeks to diminish who he made us to be.

SETTING THE RECORD STRAIGHT

Regardless of how hard we try, Jesus will *not* be domesticated. Consult the gospel facts: He is no comfortable Christ, no meek and mild Messiah.

Let's set the record straight.

Here's our popular Nice Guy misconception: Jesus didn't drink, swear, get angry, use sarcasm, confront, avoid questions, grow impatient, or complain. Conversely, the record shows he did all of the above, and the gospel includes *no* apology, confession, or repentance for any of them.

I remember chewing on one sermon that was especially hard to swallow. The minister said that Jesus didn't ingest wine because he would never consume something that had fermented or, as he put it, "putrefied." Really? If that's the case, then Jesus never ate meat either—butchered meat decomposes, even more so back then. Or do we think Jesus took bites out of living creatures?

His first recorded miracle was at a wedding in a Galilean town called Cana. He made one hundred and eighty gallons of wine for people who'd already been drinking; John tells us that "he thus revealed his glory, and his disciples put their faith in him." If he did this today, many would say he could only be a "real" Christian—he's gotta be tame—if he made and consumed grape juice. (Somehow we manage to ignore that such an act wouldn't be a miracle but an embarrassing disappointment.) We still spin-doctor to keep him in his Sunday best.

Passive Christian men must discard the belief that Jesus was perpetually mild and easy to get along with. Nice people *don't* call others a brood of vipers fit for hell (Matthew 3:7; 23:33) and "white-washed tombs" (23:27). Jesus used coarse language when being critical of authority figures. He was also irreverent and disrespectful, which are part of the definition of "profanity." We retain this caricature of Jesus being endlessly patient, yet he turned to his disciples, seemingly exasperated, and said, "How long must I be with you until you believe? How long must I put up with you?" (17:17 NLT). Jesus was *not* forever long-suffering (imagine the false agendas that would enslave him if he were—more on spotting false agendas later), and he doesn't expect his followers to be either, as seen in the parable of the fig tree (Luke 13:6–9). The clear teaching is that it's proper to wait for an unfruitful person or organization to produce, but that there's a limit to wise patience. Sometimes patience ceases to be a laudable virtue and becomes a naïve vice. Christian Nice Guys need to learn this. They would, if they saw the real Jesus.

Jesus also told us to be "wise" as serpents—some English versions render the word *phronimos* as "cunning" and others "shrewd" (Matthew 10:16). Shouldn't this make us cringe? That Christian men are supposed to be cunning and shrewd instead of nice is more proof that we just don't want to listen, or are afraid to listen, to Jesus.

Nice people don't use intense language; they're *moderate* in all they do and say. They'd never talk (literally or figuratively) about hacking off body parts that tempt a person to sin. Nice Guys don't exaggerate to prove a point. Jesus did.

Even if we begrudgingly acknowledge that he used strong words and exhibited unrefined behavior, we tend to think they must have been reserved for the corrupt and misguided religious leaders of his day. Untrue. No one, it seemed, was guaranteed safety from his ruggedness; for instance, on one occasion, his own disciples "didn't understand what he meant and were afraid to ask him about it" (Mark 9:31). Nice Guys don't generate intimidating fear; Nice Guys generate head-scratching frustration. This insipid incarnation of our own making, a cultural icon and not the real thing, wouldn't make those close to Jesus wonder if he had lost his mind and thus desire to seize him to prevent his doing damage to himself and others (3:21).

Characterless people don't use sarcasm. Jesus did. (And I thank God for it.) In fact, refusing to acknowledge that he used what I call "blessed sarcasm" spins us off into heresy. Christ shakes us awake for our own good. He loves us enough to shock us, offend us, scandalize us.

The record of his tough side is there, right there, and has been for thousands of years; his momma did *not* raise a sweet little boy. Sadly, this reality has faded into near invisibility, becoming a lost testament of sorts, what some might call a common conspiracy. The real Jesus is taking a backseat to the contemporary cultural climate, what intellectuals call zeitgeist ("spirit of the times" or "spirit of the age"). Like car keys on the kitchen table, the actual Jesus is hiding in plain view—and so is the freedom of millions, the freedom of Christian Nice Guys and those who love them.

PAUL AND STEPHEN: NO "NICE" GUYS

The Scriptures are packed with conflict, and contrary to CNG conventional wisdom, confrontation can be a path to edification, as the author of Hebrews underscores: "Let us consider one another in order to stir up love and good works" (10:24 NKJV). In translating the Greek term *paroxusmos,* the King James uses the uncomfortable word *provoke.* Similarly, Solomon, in Proverbs, states that "true love cares enough to confront" and that "better is open rebuke than hidden love" (27:5).

When Paul confronted and corrected Peter for his inconsistent and cowardly behavior toward the Gentile Christians in Antioch, Paul was engaging in this kind of edification. Previously Peter had practiced open fellowship with Gentile believers; then, when members of the ultraconservative circumcision party (Jews who believed that no one, including Gentiles, could receive salvation in Christ without being circumcised) came to Antioch from Jerusalem, he separated himself from the Gentiles in order to maintain an appearance of false orthodoxy or purity. In response to this unwarranted breaking of fellowship, Paul says, "I opposed him to his face, because he was clearly in the wrong" (Galatians 2:11). *Peter needed to be confronted, and Paul's correction actually built him up in the faith.*

Paul's letter to Philemon is crafty, clearly not the creation of a Nice Guy. Fighting for the compassionate treatment of Onesimus, a runaway slave, he cashes in some personal chips with Philemon, the owner. Paul holds Philemon hostage to his own (Paul's) past good behavior toward him (Philemon): "You owe me your very self" (v. 20). Paul sets Philemon on the meat hook; he wants him to think, *Paul was good to me—I owe him. He's compelling me to be good to Onesimus on his behalf.*

This is a shrewd move, characteristic of a good soul. A Christian Nice Guy would never have done this. A CNG would have prayed for Onesimus, slapped him on the back, and given him a supportive smile, but wouldn't have had the guts to call in such a favor. CNG's don't impose, even when it's for someone else's good and when justice is on the line. *The god and idol of a Christian Nice Guy is safety.*

Pleasant people don't say, as Paul powerfully did to Timothy, "If anyone is teaching otherwise, and will not give his mind to wholesome precepts . . . [and] to good religious teaching, I call him a pompous ignoramus" (1 Timothy 6:3–4 NEB). Earlier, Paul said to help people avoid godless myths "fit only for old women." Godless myths *aren't* fit only for old women—they also influence the minds of Christian men held up to numerous false expectations. Paul here is trafficking in a stereotype, perhaps even common slang. Yeah, it's not nice to use slang, but Paul isn't always nice; it's certainly not nice to write about a whole group of people, "Why don't these agitators, obsessive as they are about circumcision, go all the way and castrate themselves!" (Galatians 5:12 THE MESSAGE). Naughty Paul, obviously overemotional or too quick to speak; at the very least, we assume, he was in need of a reprimand.

Stephen's passionate defense of the Good News (Acts 7, especially vv. 51–53) is another excellent example of Good vs. Nice. Stephen, *"full of the*

Holy Spirit," becomes combative and tongue-lashes his audience, which furiously stones him to death. Get it? The Spirit brought him away from mere political dialogue or religious theory and into powerful confrontation. Ironically, that those he criticized "were furious and gnashed their teeth at him" in rage (v. 54) is often enough for Christian Nice Guys to conclude that the Spirit *wasn't* with him.

Power is a word frequently joined with the person and work of the Holy Spirit, and power is found not in passive malleability, but in vitality, intensity, emotional expression, will, force, action, and impetus, among other virtuous attributes; how many of these traits are men in general and Christian men in particular encouraged to exercise?

While other examples abound, I don't want to kick Nice Guy misconceptions around any more than necessary. Just know that once your CNG filters fall from your eyes, you'll see even more instances of how the early proclaimers and defenders of our faith weren't Nice Guys. God's redemptive work doesn't grow in the land of Nice. The soil can't support it.

UNCHAINED FATHER

Throughout the Old Testament, God is portrayed as a warrior, committing warfare on behalf of dependent Israel and battling against rebellious Israel. Writes Rabbi Shmuley Boteach:

> It's the Jewish nature as well to struggle and fight: the name *Israel* means "He who wrestles with G–d." We do not blithely accept injustice, plagues, or hardship. . . . It's not over until it's over, and until it's over, it's our job to fight back with every fiber in our being. (*Face Your Fear,* 151)

No wonder the American revolutionary Thomas Paine said he couldn't believe in a Judeo-Christian God—he said no religion could be divine if it contained any doctrine that offended the sensibilities of a little child. There are a lot of little Paines in church today as well, making sure Sunday sermons stay on the sweet (unbiblical) side of life—or else.

Eugene Peterson, whose *The Message* renders the entire Bible in more contemporary language, says he uses the Psalms as a means to help perplexed people approach a holy God. They don't think they're good enough to pray to him, so Peterson tells them to pray the Psalms, because they will "dispel the wrong ideas and introduce you to the real thing." The main wrong idea? The belief that the Psalms are the prayers of "nice people."

"Did you think the psalmists' language would be polished and polite?" he asks. In Hebrew, he says, the Psalms "are earthy and rough. They are not genteel. They are not the prayers of nice people, couched in cultural language." They contain "immense rage" and "terrific energies of prayer," two elements that are definitely not nice; Niceland restricts range, limits energy, and demands low-voltage living. You'll be voted out if you break these rules. (The sooner the better!)

Peterson concludes that about 70 percent of the Psalms are complaints and lamentations to God. However, you don't see many of these verses framed in Christian bookstores. They don't blend well with idyllically tender landscapes or a glowing Jesus who appears to have just received a facial.

Seventy percent of the Psalms are complaints and lamentations to God. However, you don't see many of these verses framed in Christian bookstores. They don't blend well with idyllically tender landscapes or a glowing Jesus who appears to have just received a facial.

God himself unleashed a torrent of rhetorical and sometimes sarcastic questions upon Job. Ask yourself: Are the following statements pleasant and nice?

"Why do you talk without knowing what you're talking about?"

"Where were you when I created the earth? Tell me, since you know so much!"

"Do you know the first thing about death? . . . Speak up if you have even the beginning of an answer."

"Do you presume to tell me what I'm doing wrong?"

"Do you know where Light comes from and where Darkness lives? . . . Why of *course* you know that" (a sampling from *The Message*).

You can see where Jesus got his sarcasm—his Father doesn't mince words. There's nothing mealy in his mouth.

Please notice how *Job was honest with God because he loved God.* Their relationship was passionate; he was at home in God's presence, even when he was wrong or off-base and didn't have all the answers. If we aren't honest with God, if we play games with him by hiding behind false niceness, we won't ever find out why and how we need to repent, and we will limit his rich presence and help in our lives. *Niceness is a misguided attempt to cover our lack of intimacy with God.*

Because Job loved and was honest with God, he was able to stay engaged in their relationship. Just as the experience stretched and changed him, it will likewise change you into a person of bold courage and vulnerable authenticity.

That God is not "nice" means he's not easily offended. He isn't touchy, and he doesn't make us walk on eggshells. He's direct with what he wants from us. Because God is good, he is solid and firm, so you don't have to guess what he thinks; this is the exact opposite of relating to fake nice people. We should thank him that rather than being nice, he is holy. And we should be grateful that we are not the spiritual seed of fearful men, but are the descendents of spiritual fathers who were unafraid to speak, to write, and to defend causes that then, as now, were ridiculed.

"BLESSED SARCASM"

The sarcasm of Jesus shows me just how cunning and shrewd he really is—two qualities Christian Nice Guys need to develop within (or graft into) their personality to combat pacifistic naïveté. I discovered this side of Christ's persona through the writings of C. S. Lewis and also through Elton True-blood's brilliant *The Humor of Christ,* which is subtitled "a bold challenge to the traditional stereotype of a somber, gloomy Christ." As I said before, this was an epiphany. I can tell you where I was sitting when it hit me—in my home office, before work, putting feet on a dream for a better life. Christ's sarcasm hit me between the eyes, and I laughed so hard it hurt my throat.

Not all of Christ's humor is warring and confrontational. One of the more gentle examples comes early in his ministry when he says to Simon (Peter) and Andrew, two fishermen,

"Follow me, and I will make you fishers of men" (Mark 1:17).

It's hard to think that, in response, they did not smile as we do today. This example of Christ's ironic humor is repeated often, partly because *this* instance is witty, safe, and comfortable. Other examples are far from safe, showing how humor can be wielded as a weapon of truth. Remember: Jesus says we are to follow his example.

The redemptive humor of Christ protected others from religious hypocrisy, false piety, and soul-numbing pretense. He warned that the Pharisees enjoyed putting heavy burdens upon others that they themselves refused to carry, and he combated this spiritual abuse with dripping sarcasm:

"It is easier for heaven and earth to disappear than for the least stroke of a pen to drop out of the Law" (Luke 16:17).

Put in the larger context of Christ's teaching, he clearly cannot mean that upholding the minutiae of the law is more important than the whole of heaven and earth. Rather, the *upholders* of the law were more concerned with the law than with the lives of people and a true relationship with God. Jesus' joke oozed blessed sarcasm, because he said it to protect the vulnerable from the religiously dangerous. And if we deny the use of sarcasm to drive home spiritual truth with the blunt power of a hammer, then we cannot avoid the conclusion that the early Christians who realized that God no longer requires circumcision and dietary restrictions were wrong. If what Christ said was literal, then it was simply false. *His words only make sense when we realize and acknowledge that he was being sarcastic.*

Jesus is also sarcastic in Mark 7:9, where he criticizes the Pharisees:

"You have such a *fine* way of rejecting the commandment of God" (ESV, emphasis added).

Again, we Christians have a choice: Either interpret this (and other such statements) literally and thus spin off into absurdity—Jesus compliments those who reject God's commandments?—or surrender to his obvious humor. When we see these words as righteous sarcasm, we can discover that he cares enough for us to fight for our spiritual health, and in response we then love him even more.

> "It is not the healthy who need a doctor, but the sick. I have come not to call the righteous, but sinners" (Mark 2:17).

Jesus said this to the Pharisees, his loudest critics (though far from the only ones). Think about it: Is he really saying there are two groups of people, those who need salvation and those who don't? If so, then he contradicts himself and our theology is shipwrecked. This is where we go if we strait-jacket Jesus into his Nice Boy polo shirt and refuse to accept that he shot barbed ridicule at his opponents. In essence, Christ is saying: "Sure, you guys. You're sooooo righteous—of *course* you don't need me. I've only come to rescue those poor peons you rightly look down on. Right. . . ."

A nice Jesus is a heretical Jesus.

Christ threw exaggerated humor at his own followers when they were immaturely impressed with the crowds they'd created. Jesus corrected them with, "Wherever the corpse is, there the vultures will gather" (Matthew 24:28 ESV); he was reminding them that people gather for myriad reasons, not all of which are good or fruitful. He chose to make this point by lacing it with somewhat morbid humor—vultures don't appreciate corpses, but devour them—and the gospel bears its accuracy, since there is no evidence that a single person in a crowd of five thousand men (not including women and children) who came to hear and see him then became a follower. This is a shrewd, cunning observation fortified by far more than saccharine humor, which in many churches is about the only humor tolerated.

In Christ's encounter with the Canaanite woman whose daughter was demon-possessed, his words only make sense when understood as exaggerated banter. She begged him to exorcise the girl, and, if we are to take his words only as straightforward prose, he said something contemptuous, cruel, and foul: "It is not right to take the children's bread and toss it to the dogs" (Mark 7:27 ESV). The mother, understanding the reference to women as dogs, then a cultural slur, responded, "Yes, Lord, but even the dogs under the table eat the children's crumbs" (v. 28 ESV). Due to her response—"for such a reply"—Jesus healed her daughter.

If taken at face value, says Trueblood,

> It is at complete variance from the rest of the Gospel, particularly in connection with the poor and needy. How can we square this with His acceptance of harlots and tax gatherers and His faith in poor fishermen? . . . If Christ's words . . . are wholly serious, they are a permanent stumbling block to the Gospel. But, if they represent a form of banter, which is consistent with deep compassion, they give us one of the most delightful pictures of our Lord which we possess.

Jesus called her a dog, but he didn't mean it; he was empathizing with her cultural predicament. In the larger context, he certainly was being critical, but not of the woman: against the prevailing outlook of the day, he was being pointedly critical of a culture that denigrated females. A Nice Guy can't embrace and enact this kind of courage.

Sometimes Jesus used exaggeration to shock and change minds. Do we really think Peter was possessed by the devil when Jesus told Peter, "Get behind me, Satan!"? (Mark 8:33). Many actually do, maintaining a concept of a dour, wooden, robotic Christ. Honestly though, wouldn't Mark, who transcribed Peter's recollections, have recorded the necessary exorcism of Peter *had* he been possessed? Would Jesus really have left Peter, to whom he entrusted the keys to the kingdom, in such a state? Think of the ramifications of *that*! Nice people neither exaggerate nor raise their voices—but good people do, when they're trying to shock us out of our wrongheaded thoughts and ideas.

Jesus also gave the siblings James and John the name *Boanerges,* which means "Thunder Brothers" ("Sons of Thunder"). Could it be that rather than condemning their powerful personalities Christ celebrated them with a new name to reflect who they were? We'd put such men in sensitivity training today. After all, when was the last time you saw someone asked to leave a church because he was too amiable and nice?

> **When was the last time you saw someone asked to leave a church because he was too amiable and nice?**

When award-winning humorist Greg Hartman ran a 15,000-subscriber Web site containing Christian humor, he soon ran into some baffling criticism. Wrote one woman, "How DARE you!!! I immediately deleted your site from my favorites. Tonight, I find that it DID NOT delete. Talk about being 'of the devil,' this site surely is. How you can get away with calling this 'Christian Humor' is unbelievable. My consolation is in knowing you will answer come Judgment Day."

If Hartman stands condemned, then so does Jesus. The shock will be the other way around. (All Hartman quotes from *Plain Truth* [Nov/Dec. 2004]: 29.)

Why aren't Christians more willing to use and enjoy humor—especially satire? "Lack of backbone," for one, says Hartman, who writes,

> Lord, deliver us from the sin of being too nice!
> Some people have the spiritual gift of being offended. . . . Get used to it. If we can't bring ourselves to face the possibility of offending someone, we'll never be able to consistently speak the truth. (Proverbs 27:5–6)

We also lack confidence.

> A satirist needs the guts to stand up in public, point at the actions of someone else, and—loudly—say "Wrong!" If we don't really believe God is for us (Romans 8:31), or that we have the right, if not the obligation, to warn of God's judgment against sin, we'll stay seated and silent. (John 7:24)

Nice, tame, spiritually arrogant people often don't get or appreciate sarcasm because it disrupts the status quo. *Sarcasm bothers them because it stim-*

ulates the necessary work of self-criticism, a cornerstone of moral credibility.

But blessed sarcasm does help the weak and needy. Said one subscriber to Hartman's site: "I struggle with severe chronic depression. Sometimes the only way I can get going in the morning is by reading your jokes. I just wanted you to know someone appreciates what you do." Christ loves him, you, and me enough to wield the mighty and poignant sword of sarcasm.

THE RESULT OF OUR FALSE BELIEF: WEAK LIVING

I have a non-Christian friend who says he can spot Christians at Hollywood parties: "They worship at the altar of other people's approval." He's fascinated as to why Christians think Jesus was so wimpy and gentle, when even he can read that Jesus wasn't: "Jesus is portrayed as some weak guy who patted kids on the head all the time," and it amazes him that Christian men supposedly must follow this example.

He loves Christians—*his* best friend is a Christian, so he's no bigot. When I want to disagree with him, more times than not I have to agree: Often we're the bland leading the bland. Possible ramifications of our spinelessness are dire: It can make us horrible protectors, delinquent parents.

Phil, a struggling CNG from Colorado, says he grew up believing in a Jesus who'd back down before almost anyone. "I was told that Jesus never got angry and I shouldn't either. I was taught to constantly please people, regard-

> **Christian men often are the bland leading the bland.**

less of what they were asking. I was taught not to stand up for myself." Phil told me how his life isn't what it should be, and it haunts him.

Dan, an infrequent radio caller of mine, expressed the prevalent view among evangelical men and how squeamish they are when it comes to the necessity of physical defense. When we devoted a show to whether or not a kid should stand up to a schoolyard bully, Dan called to say he believes only in "fighting with prayer." He said he's taught all his children that if someone humiliates them, the humiliation is good for them, part of God's will—they should suffer for righteousness' sake.

My co-host, Bill Gallagher, says I nearly turned purple.

"Dan," I replied, "most kids aren't being picked on at school for righteousness' sake. They're being picked on because they wear glasses, are ugly, pretty, tall, short, because their hairstyle is six months behind the fashion curve."

So let's take off the spiritual veneer. "Dan," I went on, "what would you do if your prayers went unanswered and your daughter was still being picked on by a mean boy at school?"

Dan, like so many evangelical men, actually said he'd let the humiliation continue. In some misguided notion of meekness and humility, he would allow his daughter to be beaten both physically and emotionally by a person who should be detained somewhere. This still makes me angry. She wouldn't be suffering for the Lord, for righteousness; she'd be suffering because her father's a Christian Nice Guy, a man so fearful of conflict that he hides behind a distorted misrepresentation of God to give his fear a spiritual glimmer. Imagine the abandonment his daughter would experience, the pathetic outlook she would form about men, about her father, about her Father.

Not only should we shun Dan's disguised passivity, we shouldn't rule out the option taken by the late Minnesota senator Paul Wellstone, the devoted father (and champion wrestler) who once strong-armed a neighborhood bully threatening his son. My sons and daughter have my go-ahead to defend themselves physically and verbally against bullies—even if our over-feminized public school system objects—and I've also promised to take them out to ice cream afterward. (Note that this is the same educational system where boys are shockingly falling behind—currently a silent epidemic. See Duke University's "Gender Advantage in 28 Indicator Series," Table II, 36–37, as quoted in Glen Sacks' e-mail newsletter, "Glen Attacked in *LA Times*," 3/28/05.) Life is full of suffering; there's no legitimate reason to suffer indiscriminately.

My children know that picking on them is like picking on me. They are flesh of my flesh, and trust me, this fact will be communicated with memorable clarity and intensity to *any* bully. My kids know that their father will take quick and decisive action on their behalf, even if it includes inviting the bully and his family to our house for dinner. Though I doubt the invitation would be accepted, I'm not kidding—I've told my kids about this possibility—and here's my thinking: Before I get tough with bullies and their families (being as persistent as needed, including legal action if necessary), I'm going to heap kindness on them first, because I know that kids don't really want to be bullies. They're not happy souls, and much of their unhappiness is out of their control at a young age. (Oh, how I know.) I'll try to befriend him or her first, and if the issue continues, I will travel through other areas of life's demanding spectrum. That's what Jesus did.

Whenever we're tempted to think of Jesus as a swell guy who obeyed all the rules, we should remember the Resurrection. Did you know he broke the law when he walked out of that tomb? His resurrection broke Pilate's seal over the tomb (illegal), and angels struck down government guards (*very* illegal), both federally punishable by death. Jesus, by legal definition, was a criminal, a fugitive, an outlaw, a rebel with the highest cause. Angels also partook in the criminal conspiracy, as did God the Father. As the plot thickens, it's invigorating to see how goodness fights while niceness just watches. Phenomenally, though, nice people criticize good people because the latter threaten to blow the former's cover, another reason we won't acknowledge the obvious conclusion.

Why in all our years of church and of partaking in so-called "men's ministry" have we not been told about *this* Jesus? Why do we keep *this* Jesus under wraps? Because we don't think people, especially women, will accept him.

However, my experience working with the women of CNGs tells me the opposite. They want this side of Jesus proclaimed from the rooftops, and they shout "Amen!" when I do. They know they'll get a stronger husband, boyfriend, son, or grandson when the real Jesus is set loose. We're underestimating our sisters (most of them, anyway), and we're making their lives harder.

Timid and passive Christian Nice Guys believe in a Jesus who doesn't exist except in popular imagination. Other myths stop CNGs and those who love them from joining the Good Guy Rebellion as well. Turn the page if you want to enlist.

OTHER EARNEST BUT DAMAGING CHURCH MESSAGES TO MEN

There are far more godly women in the world than there are godly men.

— COTTON MATHER

It is the age of woman-worship. Women are angels; men are demons.

— ORESTES BROWNSON

That Jesus didn't stay on the tender side of life should be apparent by now. Still, though, the false message persists and prevails that Christian men should be all hush puppies, no combat boots. Because the reasons we hold this misguided notion in our minds are both numerous and tenacious, they won't go away without a fight.

Some from within the church emanate a half-Jesus with the best of intentions, exemplified by the Christian Men's Movement of the 1990s, which reaped high attendance and short-term fervor, but had limited success in revealing Jesus' complete personality. In the real world, good intentions alone don't cut it. We need a mass infusion of common sense if men who have departed from the local church are to return. This will also help men who haven't left, but who've learned to disguise their yawns and who check their watches during sermons that cater almost entirely to feminine sensibilities and concerns.

THE SIDE EFFECTS OF TOUGH MEDICINE

The church, partially with noble motive, encourages men to deny vital parts of their masculine composition, often stored in their cooling hearts, in order to shore up our culture's crumbling families and in doing so combat our incredible rates of divorce, child neglect, and related ills.

Many thinking people, more conservative than liberal, now look back with regret upon the feminist movement and its sexual revolution. The 1960s in America helped create one of the greatest periods of gender confusion in history, and both sexes bear the blame. Many men walked away from their traditional roles of providing for and protecting women and children, and the result has been a multileveled catastrophe. Men widely misspent their masculinity, spilling semen with little concern for repercussion, a destructive shift that created an epidemic of out-of-wedlock births, which statistically leads to increased poverty, gang activity, drug abuse, family fragmentation, and an array of serious crime.

It's also helpful to admit that such revolts happen for a reason. Women long have been discriminated against in the workplace and society in general.

The most salient historical example is how women were denied the right to vote, until the ratification of the Nineteenth Amendment. Within the realm of Christian publishing I've read some mind-bending arguments trying to justify this injustice. One popular treatise is that the man of the house cast the vote for his entire household. But the Constitution doesn't refer to the right of a household to vote—it refers to individuals. Do we really think allowing a woman to vote undercuts domestic male leadership? (Amazingly, some still do.)

Even when women finally won the seventy-year-long conflict for voting rights, it wasn't without certain men's selfish motives. For the suffragist movement, the western frontier proved fertile ground for reasons as common as birds and bees: Women-starved Wyoming, where males outnumbered females six to one, was the first state to grant women full privileges in 1890. As the thinking went, *if giving women the right to vote gets them out here, so be it.* Colorado and Idaho, with their plethora of lonely silver miners, soon followed suit. Utah's Mormon men supported a woman's right to vote not because it was inalienable, but because multiple wives could vote in ways that would defend the Mormon world view.

Women's right to vote, a cornerstone of freedom and democracy, came through the side door of American politics—a hearty prejudice still stood in their way. As history shows, it takes time and strength to combat such jaundiced bias.

Dr. James Dobson says,

> There is no doubt in my mind that the [feminist] movement has brought greater respect and dignity for females, especially in the business world.
>
> Prior to 1965, it was not uncommon for an attractive young woman in the work force to be treated like a piece of flesh, a toy to be used by men. . . .
>
> In this and many related ways, the elevated self-concept of women has been a healthy phenomenon in our culture.

You don't need a political science degree to see that women have not been treated with respect. I know several in their thirties and forties whose fathers told them that "women don't go to college." Watched any reruns of *All in the Family* lately? Archie's treatment of his wife—and of women in general—isn't funny. It's disgusting. (I hope we will look back on today's sitcoms portraying men as bumbling fools with similar disdain.)

I remember a car ride with a respected elder of a local church. He told me that he agreed with the derogatory saying about women being on equal footing with dogs due to their more emotional nature. I couldn't believe what I was hearing, and I still can't believe it. This was a man who did marriage counseling.

A dear friend once told me about hunting for an apartment in the

1970s for her and her three children after her divorce. When at last she did find someone who would rent to her, she was told that "it would be best if you got rid of one of your children." Can you imagine someone saying that today?

Before the sexual revolution, men on average showed troublingly low levels of interest in the emotional lives of their wives and children. Some elements of fatherhood have improved substantially. For example, the amount of time that fathers devote to child rearing increased 170 percent between 1965 and 1998. "Men were the weak link in the home," says sociologist Bradford Wilcox, "so organizations like Focus on the Family and Promise Keepers have targeted men with messages to be more involved and exercise their unique influence."

In his classic account of the cross-cultural role fathers fulfill in societies around the world, anthropologist Bronislaw Malinowski wrote:

> The most important moral and legal rule concerning the physiological rite of kinship is that no child should be brought into the world without a man—and one man at that—assuming the role of sociological father, that is, of guardian and protector, the male link between the child and the rest of the community. . . . This generalization amounts to a universal sociological law. (*Sex, Culture, and Myth,* 169–70)

The father plays a fundamental part in fostering the well-being of his children; men haven't always taken this truth as seriously as they widely do today.

THE CHURCH'S STRONG MEDICINE TO MEN

The sexual revolution's destruction of the nuclear family is now a historical reality. Equally established is how the church fought back—one of only a handful of cultural institutions with enough guts to do so—by telling entire generations of men to take their responsibility and duty more seriously. This, in fact, has been the primary cry of churches for more than four decades: *Men, focus only upon your domestic responsibilities.* A Christian man has been told for decades that his wife's priorities should be his priorities, and the result is astounding: Evangelical wives now report higher levels of sex-life satisfaction than any other group. How evangelical men wish this was true for them as well.

> **We are over-domesticated. Men are dying inside because we've ignored a critical portion of our heart, a vital source of masculine power, courage, and bravery; in being "nice and responsible," it's as if we're living by a creed of "Let's not make things any worse than we already have."**

Christians and non-Christians alike should be grateful for this redemptive, heroic mission that has proven to be both noble and problematic. It came during a desperate time and from a church that enmeshed itself in the toil of life even as some other groups applauded the devastation, calling it progress. The church had little time to worry about the unforeseen fallout from this over-corrective message. Fighting a devouring cancer, it has used a powerful antidote, one with an unintended side effect: We are over-domesticated. Men are dying inside because we've ignored a critical portion of our heart, a vital source of masculine power, courage, and bravery; in being "nice and responsible," it's as if we're living by a creed of "Let's not make things any worse than we already have."

Here's the good news: Encouraging men in general and Christian men in particular to be better husbands and fathers is right. Substantial progress has been made, as seen in the study from the University of Virginia that found conservative evangelical fathers to rank higher than other U.S. men in most every category.

- Conservative evangelical fathers spend more time with their children, hug and praise them more, are less likely to yell at them, and commit lower levels of domestic violence than any other group in America. They are also the most active, emotionally engaged husbands and fathers in America; [their] wives report the highest levels of happiness, love and affection. (Bradford Wilcox, *Soft Patriarchs, New Men: How Christianity Shapes Fathers and Husbands*)

These superlative fathers and husbands are also more likely to discipline their children, monitor their viewing habits, and know where they are at any given time. This is why Wilcox refers to them as "soft patriarchs," for they "balance their traditional, authority-minded approach to parenting with a large measure of involvement and affection."

WOMAN WORSHIP: THE DOMESTIC CULT

Christian men *have* made amazing progress as fathers and husbands; the bad news is, in the process they've lost an integral aspect of themselves through over-domestication. Worse, they are sometimes shamed for possessing such masculine inclinations as the desire to spend time with other men and the embracing of a competitive spirit. Your average Christian guy also lives under the weight of unattainable domestic expectations put upon him by a church that leans heavily against his disposition. It's time that masculine feelings, wants, and aspirations are taken into consideration as well. It's time for a great female awakening, what Dr. Laura humorously refers to as "the proper care and feeding of husbands."

To everyone's detriment, Christian men are like poodles—once an admirable hunting dog that's been so housebroken it's now afraid to get its feet wet. Christian Nice Guys are indoctrinated to do nothing that messes with domestic tranquility. Furthermore, in most sermons, home life is portrayed as the near exclusive domain of women, who define right and wrong through feminine sensibilities and often don't understand (and, consequently, discount) masculine ways. If you examine a CNG's home, for instance, chances are you'll find that he didn't have much say in its decoration. He gets the garage (and *maybe* the den or the office) and then is commanded to keep it clean.

Worse, Christian men complain to me that their wives dismiss essential masculine desires, like regular sexual and emotional intimacy (yes, ladies, we want emotional closeness too!), as unnecessary and even perverted.

When authentic domestic tranquility, then, is *not* achieved, men are left with no real advocate within the church; as a result, God's alleged will for our lives has become far more female-oriented (domestic) than what the Bible actually says. Throw in the strangely popular notion that somehow women are intrinsically more moral and spiritual, and you've got a real mess on your hands.

I don't know how many homilies, designed to *relieve* tension between the sexes, I've sat through where the preacher depicted women in almost supernatural terms, creating even *more* tension. These ministers have redesigned our placement in the spiritual realm with God at the top, angels next, followed by women, then finally us male cretins. When women are described as a nearly exclusive source of spiritual insight and moral understanding, the warning to CNGs is clear: Don't disagree with her, don't cross her, don't disturb her groove. I couldn't help but think, *If they're truly gifted in that way, why shouldn't they lead?*

Don't we realize that such a message can easily lead to nothing better than spiritual arrogance and a misuse of power? And if it does, will that be the husband's fault too?

I call this genderism, and it's akin to racism. Skinheads and neo-Nazis order their moral hierarchy of people based upon ethnicity, contending that some races are better than others; their prejudice offends all but a radical fringe. Yet simultaneously we let another such sinister perspective slip by us and into us at church, a prejudice veneered by a spiritual façade: We categorize human virtue based upon gender, which is morally neutral—men and women are *equally* fallen, sinful, and forgivable. Like racism, genderism leads to mockery, assault, bias, and injustice. And, like racism, genderism strips people—men, in this case—of identity and dignity.

A person can acknowledge and appreciate the *differences* between the sexes without giving in to the error of believing that one is in any sense *better* than the other. For example, women place more focus upon some areas of life than men do, such as interpersonal relationships; they have a leg up on us there, and we're foolish if we don't listen to their astute perception and wisdom in that regard.

On the other hand, fathers are more inclined to compel their children to confront life's realities at a younger age; they want their sons and daughters to learn life's lessons earlier so as to help insure healthy and independent living. As long as this introduction to the weight of life isn't too heavy, it's a good inclination that women should embrace rather than fight or undermine; otherwise, children tend to grow up anxious and unsure of their abilities.

Regardless, what does any of this have to do with women being intrinsically more spiritual? The placement of this gender-based divide into our spirituality, and the related granting of de facto superiority to women over men, illustrates how the church's pervasive genderism is spiritually and emotionally dangerous to the docile, subservient Christian husband who, under such weight, is not inclined ever to confront or question his wife on anything, no matter how lovingly. For many, the experience of genderism's heavy-handedness goes back even farther than their adult life in the church, for many evangelical mothers misguidedly attempt to drive God-given masculine desires out of their young boys.

How did we come largely to embrace genderism against the witness of scriptural teaching? The Bible constantly addresses spirituality and morality; *nowhere* does it state or imply that either women or men are more spiritual or moral than the other. I'm with the apostle Paul on this one: *All are equal in Christ Jesus* (Galatians 3:28 THE MESSAGE).

Contrary to what we say in church, notes Wilcox, women run our homes; it has been a near ironclad fact in most homes throughout world history that women are the emotional power that drives the household. As the saying goes, "If Mama ain't happy, ain't nobody happy." The church should encourage wives to use this power justly, which means sharing this strength with their husbands rather than for verbal flaunting or for emotional blackmail.

THE SPIRIT OF MS. MONITOR

On any given Sunday you can expect to find Ms. Monitor. (*Ms.,* not Mrs.—because no guy in his right mind would marry her.) She wears a darling hat perched on short, uptight hair. Her lips are pursed, her eyes eagle-like, her white-gloved fingers very busy pointing and taking copious notes on others' behavior. She makes sure we follow rules that even Jesus told us to lose.

She has no sense of humor or appreciation for paradox, around which much of spiritual life revolves. She mistakes dourness for holiness. You won't know her by her love but by her artificial conventions and man-made convictions; she represents the error warned of by Isaiah and Jesus; her "teachings are but rules taught by men" (Mark 7:7). Nothing divine or faith-inspiring comes from Ms. Monitor. She ensures that everything goes smoothly, that we never broach the edges of our comfort zones.

Ms. Monitor is femininity gone bad, just as violent men are masculinity gone bad. Most women don't trust her either—they know she's a double-agent. So why have we for so long listened to her? Because she's a product of the principalities and powers of this world, a force we must struggle against and overcome. Unless we call this what it is, her power will be permitted to endure.

THE HUSBAND IS ALWAYS TO BLAME

> A CNG husband has been enslaved to the notion that if his wife isn't happy—for whatever reason—then it's up to him to fix it. •

Domestic happiness is a delicate matter made worse in books for Christian men by messages that appear reasonable but don't work in real life. For example, though a husband has some influence regarding his wife's happiness (and vice versa), this influence has been over-blown. A CNG husband has been enslaved to the notion that if his wife isn't happy—for whatever reason—then it's up to him to fix it. In fact, he's at fault if he doesn't, even though the idea that one person can actually make another happy contradicts real-life experience. How I wish more women would admit that this sort of thinking is a tyranny for men. Writes Angela Thomas,

In the effort to make things perfect, a woman can beg her man to be like [other perfect men who don't exist]. She's hoping that if he could change then she'd finally be whole.

When the man feels like he is asked to be something he wasn't ever made to be, when he senses the pressure to meet expectations that seem unattainable . . . then the man can step back in frustration. (*The Question Every Woman Asks*)

But he's far more than frustrated. When up against such unattainable demands, and especially if his wife is immature and selfish, he doesn't just step back; he goes underground, where his masculine power always gets misspent. His desire to be active and proactive is diverted from healthy releases to perverted ones. He resents her but hides it, unsure that he can acceptably share it anywhere, especially at church, the very community from which such unrealistic expectations emanate.

Dobson says that men are saddled with unrealistic expectations:

Any sadness or depression that a woman might encounter is [allegedly] her husband's fault. At least, he has the power to eradicate it if he cares enough. In other words, many American women come into marriage with unrealistically romantic expectations which are certain to be dashed. Not only does this orientation set up a bride for disappointment and agitation in the future, it also places enormous pressure on her husband to deliver the impossible. (*Love Must Be Tough*)

The church's good message for men to become better husbands and fathers has gone too far, again with the best of intentions. One bestselling Christian author said that in thirty years of marriage counseling, he never saw one case where he believed the man wasn't at fault for the divorce; he argues that women instinctively "know when their attitude is wrong," while men are dishonest about their wrong attitudes.

This convenient fiction is void of common sense and, worse, bears false witness against millions of husbands and an entire gender. "This [expletive] message that men are always to blame for their marriage problems almost killed mine," one man told me. When he stopped going to a Christian counselor known for this teaching, his relationship with his wife improved.

I know that counselor. He no longer teaches the Christian-husband-is-always-to-blame message. He's finally acknowledged the damage, and he experienced it himself when his own marriage came apart.

When I asked a man in the midst of a divorce why it was happening, he repeated an answer marinated in this kind of thinking: "Because I'm not the man God wants me to be."

I shocked him. "That's a cop-out. No husband does it right all the time. You're basically saying that unless you're perfect, you're bound for divorce."

I said that no husband is the man God wants him to be—and if that's required, right now, then we're all in trouble—but that this wasn't the source of his problem. "Your wife didn't marry Jesus. She married you."

Sometimes men actually use impossible-to-fulfill expectations as a way of avoiding both responsibility and the real issues. But this is the exact pressure many churches put on men today. This man got it from the same church I attended until I finally grew sick and tired of the message's false premises and undeniable naïveté. I highly recommend that CNGs (1) attend churches that do not preach this message, (2) stop reading books that do, and (3) memorize these words by Dobson as a way to immunize themselves: "Marital conflict always involves an interaction between two imperfect human beings who share the responsibility to one degree or another" (*Love Must Be Tough*).

Angela Thomas notes how easily the falsehood can be used against men:

> A woman can begin to believe that a man might just be all that she needs. *He will answer my questions. He can heal my wounds. He can fill up the cup of my soul. He can make me whole.* But she has lost sight of the design: God has made us for Himself. (*The Question Every Woman Asks*)

Men are finally pushing back. After reading my related articles in *New Man* magazine, guys have told me they've had it with men being blamed for any problem that takes place in marriage and in society in general. One particularly frustrated man lamented: "Men are responsible for every problem in their homes, even when it's out of their control. If tragedy hits their home, they are told that the reason why is because they didn't lead like they should and that they didn't pray enough. It's unfair, and it's not even in the Bible!"

I've been in the church for more than twenty-five years now. I've had long talks there, I've had other long talks over dinner in members' homes, and I've noticed some patterns. For one, some of the Christian wives say nothing about God personally—going to church is about family, about family values. I'm all for family values, don't get me wrong. But I'm left with the sinking feeling that their real motive for going to church is so that man of theirs will "get his act together." If this is true, church isn't about an intimate relationship with God, but about keeping Christian men in line, which is to say, domesticated, by female standards. Men will start going back to church when this mindset is called what it is: manipulation.

THE IDEAL CHRISTIAN MAN: GIVE EVERYTHING, EXPECT NOTHING

Christian men have been directed to sacrifice in needless, unhelpful ways. Essentially, they've been told to become responsible mules, expecting nothing in return for their labor and dedication except the satisfaction of knowing they've done it. Real life doesn't work this way, not for very long at least.

Christian men tell me they are glad to sacrifice for their families, but they don't think such sacrifice should include killing themselves at jobs they can't stand so their wives can feel happy in a new car every three years and a larger home every five. They feel driven toward something more adventurous and in line with their God-given gifts, but they sense that they are enslaved to providing needless material domestic luxuries. (Christianity is packed with seemingly irresponsible behavior; for instance, it's a faith where men drop a lifelong trade, without two weeks' notice, an instant after being invited into a new and nebulous line of work. [See Mark 1:16–20.])

> It is foolish and damaging *not* to require respect in a marriage relationship; respect is a fundamental building block of all healthy connection. Interpersonally, those who don't mandate respect are among the most unattractive people.

The following profound proverb that warns against withholding the fruit of one's labor is sometimes quoted in church, but never in regard to a man's true longings: "Do not muzzle an ox while it is treading out the grain" (Deuteronomy 25:4). The context is antiquated—when was the last time you even saw an ox?—but the concept isn't. The clear teaching here is that *it's an innate desire of those who work to benefit from their labor. People long for their sacrifices to be noticed by those for whom they make the sacrifices.* Specifically, no one in his right mind goes into a marriage expecting little or nothing in return, even though this is exactly what Christian men have been told to expect. (We'll later examine an extreme view of sacrifice.) We've been encouraged to be more like butlers than true leaders. But hey—even butlers get paid!

It is foolish and damaging *not* to require respect in a marriage relationship; respect is a fundamental building block of all healthy connection. Interpersonally, those who don't mandate respect are among the most unattractive people. Christian Nice Guys don't need to give their wives any more reason to look down on them.

CNGs already face the world with timorous hearts and anxious minds. They're already predisposed to living small, and sometimes they attend undercutting churches that encourage them to live even smaller. Another false message they may hear from the church is that living a purpose-driven life is actually sinful—"living larger," allegedly, is code language for "being worldly," an errant teaching described by Stephen Strang in *Old Man, New Man: Closing the Gap Between the Life You Could Live and the Life You Are Living.* Strang grew up among Christians in suspended animation and arrested development:

In an attempt to stay in the bull's-eye of God's will, they remained in neutral. If you had any ambitious goals, they were thought to be your own desires, not God's. Those folks never accomplished a lot, but they were certain they were in God's will.

CNGs don't accomplish much either.

These are the church people I grew up around as well, people who believed that the Christian's highest aim is personal piety and impeccable manners. I also noticed that their lives didn't really amount to much, that they could have been greater and grander for God. They lived in a somewhat frozen state due to their fear of sinning (or was it fear of life in general?), neutralized by the idea that God would rather have them be immobile and static than move forward and risk tripping up. Deeper love was rare, and freedom was nonexistent. Their goal appeared to be comfort, not purpose.

AMERICA'S FEMINIZED FAITH

America's feminized Christianity has a drawn-out and somewhat complicated history. While in the 1700s *congregations* were feminized, in the 1800s *Jesus* was (Stephen Prothero, *American Jesus*, 56) and still remains so today.

During the 1700s, women were increasingly upheld as the guardians of Christian virtues; men were regarded as far less virtuous, partially because economic provision demanded aggression and competition. "There are far more godly women in the world than there are godly men," said Cotton Mather. Though not everyone agreed, contrarian voices went largely unheard. More than fifty years later, Orestes Brownson would say that era was "the age of woman-worship. Women are angels; men are demons."

Because women were seen as morally and spiritually superior, the societal prizing of their influence became imbalanced; this, of course, included the church. Said Frances Trollope, "I never saw or read of any country where religion had so strong a hold upon the women, or a slighter hold upon the men [as in America]" (in *American Jesus*, 58). No wonder this was the time where with increasing frequency we find Jesus described almost entirely in terms such as "pious and pure, loving and merciful, meek and humble." After all, if a society buys the fallacy that *women* are morally and spiritually superior, then eventually Christ must undergo drastic cultural hormone therapy too. We saw earlier that one objector to this nonsense was Charles Haddon Spurgeon, who said, "There has got abroad a notion, somehow, that if you become a Christian you must sink your manliness and turn milksop."

The popular artwork of that era confirms it. One painting called "Christ Walking on the Sea" is particularly hard to stomach. Jesus still rescues Peter from troubled waters, but it's hard to see how—he's posed as if he's doing a slow samba, living a charmed life that would never include doing anything to be convicted of sedition and executed by crucifixion. His cloak looks like a shawl (V-neck and all), as if he bore cleavage. His large maternal hips sway to his left, as though rather than saving Peter he's about to flirt with him. In fact, he's portrayed as so matronly that he appears less likely to grab Peter as to give birth.

Horace Bushnell, an influential theologian of the time, described Christ in mostly feminine terms. He compared Jesus' development to the "unfolding of a flower," his childhood "a kind of celestial flower." His youth was a "sacred flower" emitting "a fragrance wafted on us from other worlds." Upon dying, he was a "bruised flower drooping on his cross." He was "a perfectly harmless being, actuated by no destructive passions, gentle to inferiors, doing ill or injury to no one," the embodiment of the "passive virtues." (What was this guy smoking?)

In terms of status, Bushnell was the Dr. Phil of his time, his culture's primary male "advice giver." He wrote advice manuals and children's books that translated his view of an effeminate Christ into popular culture. Women were to emulate Gentle Jesus *and* teach their sons to do the same. In other words, the image stuck.

During the 1900s, Christians married Christ's male gender to a heavy dose of femininity. Women were creating a version of Jesus that they wanted men to copy: "In sermons and novels, prayers and hymns, lithographs and half-tones, evangelical and liberal Protestants alike depicted Jesus as a feminine male—what we now call an androgyne" (*American Jesus,* 85). Such a person would *not* garner allegiance from or be followed by men, in his day or ours. He would garner their irritation.

Some flat-out creepy writing from female Catholic writers hasn't helped either. Such prose revolves around what's called the Sacred Heart of Jesus, some of it stemming back to medieval times, but still enjoying an audience today. St. Gertrude referred to Christ as "my sweetest little Jesus." Another wrote of her revelation about Christ, her "Divine Spouse," who showed her that "He was the most beautiful, the wealthiest, the most powerful, and most perfect and the most accomplished among all lovers." Jesus allowed her to linger upon "His Sacred Breast, where he disclosed to me the marvels of His love and the inexplicable secrets of His Sacred Heart. . . . He kept me for two or three hours with my lips pressed to the Wound of His Sacred Heart." How I wish I were making this up, this Gospel According to St. Harlequin.

Such feminization was met with a backlash during the late 1800s and early 1900s, when influential men such as novelist Henry James complained that "the whole generation is womanized; the masculine tone is passing out of the world." No wonder a 1920 YMCA study determined that U.S. churches were only one-third male: "Roughly, three million men were missing from the pews."

At long last, progress began to manifest itself. A more accurate and masculine Christ was allowed out of the cultural closet as the twentieth century advanced. In a 1948 piece called "Not Frail, Not Pale," *Time* magazine quoted a man who was repulsed by the "sissified" image of Christ presented in Sunday school. Jesus was a "teacher's pet . . . a pale and posturing person" with "silky hair" and "an expression of simpering vapidity." The popular image of Christ was "as ugly as a rented bowling shoe."

This progress continued only until it was beat back by the feminist revolt, the negative aspects of which we still battle today. Feminism may have started off seeking equality for women, but it soon degenerated into attacking the very soul of men, shaming men for their "abusive" and "destructive" nature. For example, in a speech entitled "Men: Natural-Born Killers," renowned feminist Dr. Helen Caldicott said that men harbor an unbridled bloodlust—they have a "killing reflex" located in their brain. That women also violently abuse children is a fact she doesn't address; men, she asserts, are "almost clinically and psychologically dead."

I thought about Caldicott's assertions while watching the much-televised Scott Peterson trial. After Peterson was convicted on two counts of first-degree murder, a crowd outside the California courthouse waited for the jury's recommendation: life in prison, or death. When the answer came down—death—they cheered. Called others on their cell phones. Mugged for the cameras. Smiled and applauded. According to Caldicott's theory, this group wanting Scott Peterson to be killed by the state should have been largely or fully comprised of men. But it wasn't. There were about as many women applauding the verdict. And seven women were on that jury. If such a "bloodlust" and "killing reflex" does exist, then both genders seem to have it.

Feminism, which became a multifaceted revolution that attacks the very masculine heart, has been driven by such extremists as the one who wrote that masculinity hinders men from worshiping God. "Taking up the cross, denying himself, and abasing himself before God is hardly the fulfillment of his [man's] masculinity!"

Masculinity, therefore, must be evil: "Pride in independence thus appears as a Satanic device for keeping men from faith in Christ." The answer? "Only if men become like women can they become Christian" (Leon Podles, *The Church Impotent*, 36). *We may deny this statement in theory, but we embrace it as a matter of practice.*

TAKING EPHESIANS TOO FAR

Christian men have been held hostage by the misappropriation of certain directives in Paul's letter to the troubled Ephesians. Ephesus was known for believers with sound doctrine but cold hearts, and Paul admonished them to be *more* humble, gentle, patient, loving—to live in "all humility and gentleness, with patience, bearing with one another in love" (4:2 ESV). This oft-quoted text has been used to hammer Christian Nice Guys "into shape," but not the right shape. Ironically, misapplication of key words and phrases in the very next chapter, Ephesians 5, has caused suffering for Christian wives regarding false interpretations of marital submission.

When Paul wrote this epistle, Ephesus was the most prominent city in Asia Minor, the cultural and economic hub of the region, cosmopolitan, widely tolerant of diverse ideas. However, the temple of the goddess Artemis (Seventh Wonder of the World) was a looming presence both religiously and economically; apparently there wasn't much tolerance for exclusivistic religious claims that were seen to threaten the industries dependent on the dominant goddess cult (see Acts 19).

No doubt a church planted in this environment of competing ideas would be committed to defending and promoting the purity of the gospel. Often when people become zealous for orthodoxy, they tend toward insensitivity, harshness, and ungraciousness in their attitudes toward others; this seems to have happened in Ephesus. Paul's letter contains no doctrinal correction, but he gives clear instruction regarding the Spirit-filled life and relational behavior (5:15–6:9). Also, in John's Revelation, Christ says to the Ephesian church, "I have this against you, that you have abandoned the love you had at first" (2:4 ESV).

Apparently, the Ephesians were theologically discerning and passionate in their fight against the perversion of truth, but they frequently violated the spirit of grace and selfless love they were also called to express. By doing this, they were giving a distorted witness to Christ's character and nature, what John's gospel (1:14) calls the perfect expression of grace *and* truth. (Christian Nice Guys do exactly the opposite: They are gracious, but refuse to take up the sword of truth.) The Ephesians were called to repent and return to the "love [they] had at first" by doing the works they did at first (Revelation 2:5). This lack of love was not representative of everyone in the congregation, but it did reflect the general attitudes of the church's leadership (to whom Jesus specifically addressed the Revelation passage).

Taking Paul's admonition to be gentle and applying it to the entire life of a passive person—or congregation, for that matter—spells disaster. It's not only unwise, it also makes no sense when held up with confirmation by comparison with other scriptural passages. For example, if Paul meant for all people to behave gently at all times, why did he encourage Timothy to be bolder? Because, wise man that he was, he encouraged diverse behaviors based upon different situations and temperaments. (And this is the antithesis of what cult leaders advocate: Simplify the world, and your role in it, to toxic extremes.) Anyway, taking Paul's admonishment to its illogical conclusion would mean Christian guys could not be policemen, attorneys, apologists, judges—any profession or calling that demands conflict on behalf of justice. Behold the madness of niceness! No C. S. Lewis, G. K. Chesterton, Martin Luther, Martin Luther King Jr., Pope John Paul II, Fyodor Dostoyevsky, Mother Teresa, Aleksandr Solzhenitsyn, Dorothy Day, Chuck Colson, Thomas Merton, or Dietrich Bonhoeffer, among many others. Healthy debate with, and confrontational love toward, wives and children would be out of the question too.

A THIN UNDERSTANDING OF PARADOX

As broached in chapter 1, it would be so much easier and cleaner if the Christian Nice Guy problem were solely the fault of the church's good intentions. But the problem goes deeper. We need to advance our reasoning skills so we can obtain additional insight into ourselves and into God.

We sometimes don't recognize paradox or tension in the Bible or, for that matter, with life in general. *Good people are both gentle and rugged, depending on the circumstance.* There's no incongruity here.

Nevertheless, we struggle with this fact similarly to how we can't get our mind around how God is both merciful and wrathful. Accordingly, we often reside in one camp or the other, failing to see that this tension is not contradictory, but rather is vital to our spiritual lives.

When we release and reject this tension, we spin into absurdity. We get a Softy Savior and a Father who either doesn't really care about what we do, doesn't have the power to truly help us with our struggles, or, in unappeasable anger, forces us to play untenable and unwinnable charades with life. In our confusion and frustration, we pretend to be pious and then hide behind heartless dogma.

Our belief about God tends to center around our inclinations. If we don't care for a God who wants us to face our fears, then we gravitate toward a hush-puppy Jesus who longs to catch a groovy wave with us—surf's up! If we think we're pretty hot stuff and that sinning is something other people do, we hook onto the wrathful-God model.

A solid example of this tension being workable and beneficial is seen in how love is both flexible and rigid. A good father is flexible while handling the folly of a small child, but he's rigid when he finds out that this once-infantile kid is taking life-threatening drugs as a teenager. He is good in both these situations. Even if this behavior on the surface seems to contradict itself, upon further examination we find it to be true and right. That is the definition of paradox. Good people travel the entire healthy behavioral spectrum, just as Christ did.

There *are* legitimate reasons to be concerned about a message that tells men to embrace their entire masculine nature, from gentle to rugged. As history shows, so much masculine energy can easily go astray and lead men into typical male vices, such as damaging violence and brooding autonomy. What we fail to acknowledge, however, is that history also shows how lives go bad when men don't embrace this full range. Europe's refusal to help millions of Jews during World War II is the most stunning example that comes to mind. Neutering masculinity is the largest oversight of the gender war and of the church's noble battle within it throughout the last forty years.

Somewhere along the way in this bloody and valiant culture war, the church abandoned some common sense between the sexes. We've shot at our own men, a theological/sociological form of friendly fire. I know the torment that worms through the heads of such victims—they trust me and so they talk to me. They're livid with the church, and while at first I didn't know what to say, now I do. You're reading it.

> **When we're free from the myths that Jesus is the Supreme Nice Guy, that the Father is a cosmic teddy bear, and that the Holy Spirit is a docile, breezy presence, men will find the church more compelling and relevant.**

When we're free from the myths that Jesus is the Supreme Nice Guy, that the Father is a cosmic teddy bear, and that the Holy Spirit is a docile, breezy presence, men will find the church more compelling and relevant, and Christian Nice Guys will begin to see the world more clearly. They will be better-equipped agents of redemption. Life-draining naïveté is among the first ailments to go, which should cheer our hearts, since Christ told those who followed him not to be naïve (Matthew 10:17), and Paul warned against naïveté as well (2 Timothy 3:1).

CHILDHOOD, WHERE WE LEARNED TO LIVE SMALL

I hated life.

—ECCLESIASTES 2:17

God did not give us a spirit of timidity.

—PAUL, TO TIMOTHY, HIS ANXIOUS STUDENT (2 TIMOTHY 1:7)

"Those who learn from their suffering, God delivers from their suffering."

—JOB 36:15 THE MESSAGE

Though the Christian Nice Guy problem affects every man who attends your average church, it's harder on some than others. This is because some men are more predisposed to passive thinking, and it's not rocket science to figure out why: Fear and related emotions like anxiety have too much influence over them. Though fear and anxiety are the lower back pain of our spiritual lives—who hasn't experienced them?—their woundedness is extraordinary.

If excessive passivity haunts you or someone you love, know that you weren't "born this way." You may or may not have endured a time of prolonged and traumatic abuse, as I did; there are other paths that can lead just as surely to overarching passivity in your adult life. If you live under the influence of fear and anxiety, then something went wrong, somewhere along the line, and it's time to address the question marks that burden you.

NOWHERE TO HIDE

Fundamental episodes of my childhood were a confusing mixture of conditional acceptance and profound abuse. I was a Nice Guy just waiting to happen.

My mother hit, slapped, battered, and humiliated me more times than I can remember. She seemed to get a special rush of supremacy out of doing so in public. She was indignant if I dared to defend myself, so I learned to relax, to roll with the blows much like a stuntman. This way the beatings were shorter; more intense, but shorter.

The best way to describe what it felt like is through the events of the film *Saving Private Ryan,* especially the beginning, when Allied fighters storm the beaches of Normandy. The camera shakes violently, as I was shaken violently—there was no stopping the attack. Soldiers drown in the tidal waters, as I drowned emotionally on land. The thunderclaps of battle make young men lose their minds, as the verbal assaults scattered my thoughts as well. Terror has them in its grip, reducing them, and reducing me, to human rubble.

Though I could fill this book with scenes from my past, the following are a few dramatic lowlights.

I was thrown across the kitchen by my hair, slamming into cabinets, hitting the cold linoleum, wetting myself, then living with that heavy shame. I couldn't walk after being cracked across my lower back with a long vacuum cleaner attachment. I escaped further beatings by dragging my limp lower body up the stairs with my forearms and elbows, the way soldiers crawl under barbed wire in boot camp.

Among the most frightening moments came when I'd return home from elementary school. Mother, prone to emotional meltdowns, would stand on the front porch, cigarette in her right hand, left hand clutching the black iron railing. She was a human gate who stood tall for a short woman, electrified by a perverse power. The look in her eyes was the same as on the men who beat Jesus in *The Passion of the Christ* . . . sadistic pleasure. *See what I get to do to you today,* it guaranteed. The first blow sometimes landed before I could scramble through the door. I found myself face down many times. I still remember the metallic taste of blood.

Here's what most people do with such accounts: They focus on the physical stuff and think that's where the difficulty begins and somehow ends, when our body's defenses get to work and clean up the evidence. We think, *His lip is no longer split—he's okay.* This is the same tidy and convenient theory I tried to get myself to believe too. I know better now.

I'll tell you straight: Along with physical pain comes a message and a messenger. Upon that floor, the grim reaper of self-loathing lay upon me like a full-contact fighter in the octagon. Self-reproach smashed my nose into the pee of my worthless self. It wanted me to hate myself and to distrust others, especially that God up there.

This monstrous, sweaty beast on my back held court on me, and I couldn't win. I eventually gave up and confessed, *I'm guilty of all he says. I'm valueless.* My intuition sensed a conspiracy, but I couldn't prove anything; it was all so overwhelming. How does a kid beat such a bad rap, especially when he agrees with accusations of such evil? To whom does a young boy run?

Church folk? They didn't seem to possess any rescuing power. They mostly smiled and kept to themselves the way "good folk" should.

Neighbors? Are you kidding? This was the '70s. Kids were to be seen, not heard.

Jesus? Again, my catechism Jesus was always shattered by my sin, for which he was constantly having to re-sacrifice himself, and he was exhausted. I kept saying "sorry," but my boyhood sins kept driving more wedges, or so I was told. We could never get close.

Teachers? I couldn't tell if they liked me, and anyway, Mom played a cunning game with them. She used her political face, voice, and that charming Irish laugh the same way squid deploy ink: to keep them off her trail.

But wait a second. There *was* someplace I could go: into my head. I could create an alternative universe and even change the definitions of things, the way I saw adults doing, deceptively pretending not to experience or even notice realities. If I jettisoned the part of me that felt emotions, I might be able to get rid of anguish, humiliation, self-loathing, despair. I could learn not to wince and cry when I felt pain so the pounding and the yelling would end more quickly. I could charm my abuser, tell her what she wanted to hear: "I'm stupid. I'm always doing dumb things." I could learn not to demand much and, most important, keep my thoughts to myself. I could take my life and tone it down, get under the radar. I could go passive, numb, apathetic.

Corrie ten Boom had her hiding place. So did I.

Strategy. We've all got one.

What did I do wrong, go to school? I'd wonder after the attacks. I don't remember any *Honey, how was your day?* moments back then.

Other times when I'd find her in the same place (the porch) with the same intimidating position, I couldn't tell from her indifferent expression what she was going to do next. Her hugs and her hits came from the same baffling source. I entered my home the way a marine enters buildings in Iraq: tentatively, and with pounding heart. No wonder I didn't do much homework; I had survival on my mind.

It may sound weird, but you get used to physical beatings—like meals, they become part of your "normal" day. Though it's unpredictable knowing when they will begin, they take on a familiar pattern once they commence. You try to shut down your emotions the best you can and simply absorb the onslaught. (Sadly, you become so proficient that you shut down the good feelings too.) The first blows are the worst; then your attacker fatigues. (Thank God she didn't work out.)

Welts relax. Skin rejuvenates and bones mend. It was her words that contained such longevity. That's where the damage settled, festered, and consumed.

"They are coming for you in two hours because you're such an evil boy," she told me more than once.

They were the unnamed strangers, her make-believe agents of judgment, who were going to take me away from my family forever to some sinister location due to my unforgivable little-boy transgressions like being too loud or having an opinion that differed from hers. She would say these words while staring down at me with large, furious eyes and lips that would suddenly turn up at the ends and smile. My mental anguish gave her an unnatural high. Then the countdown began in earnest. She savored these words:

"They're coming for you in an hour and a half. . . ."

"They're coming for you in an hour. . . ."

"They're coming for you in half an hour. . . ."

"They'll be here any minute to take you away because you're such an *evil* boy."

Though Mom screamed a lot, these pronouncements came out slow and thick. She glared these heavy words into me with a cruel pleasure.

She kept a pile of shoes and other objects near her favorite spot on the living room couch; that way, when I would come through the door later in the day, she could grab them quickly and throw them at me (right-handed).

I learned how to handle it. I timed the sprint to my room. I'd take five steps or so, then hit the hardwood on my belly, making sure to maintain my home-plate slide. When the projectiles would crash against the wall above my head, I would get up and run before she could reload. She'd curse at me with filthy words, then cough out an arrogant laugh that seemed to choke back her conscience. Once behind the door, I would stay in my room, not knowing whether Round Two was coming, and all the while wondering, *What did I do? Who am I, really?*

I was left alone with maternal madness. Dad was a house painter who often worked seven days a week for weeks on end. He provided well, but was frequently unresponsive. My parents were first-generation immigrants to America, so there was no extended family for me to run to. No neighbor showed a rescuing nature. They were what all neighbors should be: nice.

I was trapped by this insanity and a part of me recognized it. I told myself I wasn't evil, that I was being lied to. I fought to keep my soul together the way a pilot struggles to keep a flaming aircraft from crashing. I gripped the controls of my life, but the plane was too big. Steering is hard enough as an adult, and as a young boy my hands were too little, my mind insufficiently wise-as-a-serpent for this task. I fought and fought but still couldn't discern the horizon. Failure was inevitable.

Mother relished my struggles and mocked my tears, saying they were illegitimate and groundless—another message that there was something intrinsically wrong with me.

She ridiculed me when I tried to escape her dark proclamations. How dare I exert my will, disagree, use my skills, retain my dignity and value? Stunningly, I would later receive similar criticism from portions of the church.

Wiping away the venom of her words by telling her I wasn't evil only made life harder. Her fury spiked to new and more vicious levels. I couldn't win. I was called every vile, demeaning name in the book, including some foreign ones I had to look up later in life. It didn't matter, because such spoken assaults, such vicious prophecies, reveal the same verdict: *You are a void stripped of identity.*

That boys are often emotionally fragile and afraid of the world is one reason they participate more in the martial arts. (As an aside, it kills me when people say boys enter martial arts to learn greater discipline. What young boy wakes up and says, "I've given it a lot of thought, Pops, and I see now that I need more discipline in my life. Let's try martial arts"? Discipline is a by-product, not a motive.) *Boys often wonder if they have what it takes to make it.* According to my mother's real but (I believe) unintentional message, I didn't have to wonder: I was worthless. I'd never amount to anything. So give up now.

You can see that this wasn't discipline, but destruction. I learned to say nothing, to show no emotion, so she couldn't shred more parts of me. I learned to die among the living.

You're wrong, Mom! I inwardly rampaged. But I made my face deceive and say, *It's okay. This doesn't hurt me.* I remember thinking I'd be better off if I did live with mysterious strangers, and I felt the hole that this sickening realization carved inside me; foreign, an unjust invasion against God's good plans for me. It's a desperate thought for a young boy to recognize against his nature that strangers might treat him better than his own mother. It would be much later when I could echo the words of the courageous martyr (and Christian *Good* Guy) Stephen: *I forgive you. You didn't know what you were doing.*

I eventually found out that my mom's father was tough on her as a girl. Abuse (like high cholesterol) tends to run in families, holding generations in bondage. Family histories aren't much different than national ones: when you're ignorant of them, you're bound to repeat the same mistakes. Facing a family heritage is

> **Evil tries to completely disintegrate your comprehension of yourself—to rob you of your existence.**

difficult, but liberating, because there's no law that says you have to continue down the same errant path. We can endeavor to create a better now and a brighter future.

Back to my boyhood. Life lost more and more mystery; again, childhood wonder is a luxury when survival's on the line. I learned to become no one, nowhere. My God-given healthy spirit limped along in hiding. I entered the wacky world of passivity, a haunted house I'd never intended to roam. Worse, fight as I did, some venom made its way into me, ensuring that my journey out of the submissive Christian Nice Guy world would be even more arduous.

And isn't that the goal of our soul's enemy? To get us to think either too much (pride and arrogance) or too little (self-hatred and self-loathing) about ourselves? That we aren't made in God's majestic image and so we don't matter? I have seen evil and I know its ploy: to steal your personhood, your singular God-given identity. Evil tries to completely disintegrate your comprehension of yourself—to rob you of your existence.

I know that if you had markedly different experiences, it's difficult to empathize with some of what I'm writing. If this applies to you, sometimes it helps to remember how you felt when you went without sleep for a length of time. Remember how hard it was to control your mind? How wild your thoughts could become? How you murmured and complained about things you normally wouldn't have mentioned?

Vince Lombardi said, "Fatigue makes cowards of us all." You go into hiding. People who have been tortured with sleep deprivation speak of how they lost a sense of who they were, and about the resultant hopelessness. They say it was like someone else took over their mind. Now imagine that "no one, nowhere" feeling for more than a night or two—for weeks, month, years.

I derive no pleasure from this kind of writing. My throat tightens as I recall those days; I sip hot coffee, but it won't release. I turn up the Cowboy Junkies, but they don't drive away the feelings either. Yeah, it hurts, but that doesn't stop me anymore. It's no longer a crushing kind of hurt, the kind that paralyzes. I pray when I think of these and other moments because they were real, and I'm thankful they are no more.

I used to be the editor of a weekly newspaper, which means there's a somewhat detached and skeptical journalist alive and well in me. As such, penning a sort of *Mommy Dearest* chapter is contrary to my inclination. And please know that my childhood wasn't bad 24/7. There were loving moments, also, though they often came with a worrisome wondering: *How long will this mood last?*

Lives don't go wrong from too much love and affection. I'm revealing all this to you because it helps us get to the root of the Nice Guy problem.

Crippling passivity can also come from sources other than physical, emotional, or sexual abuse. For instance, it can originate from at least one controlling or hyper-concerned parent (often a domineering, controlling mother aided by an absent or weak father). Overprotection may play a role, as can excessive demands and mixed reactions of acceptance and hostility.

Spiritual abuse is an underreported cause as well. When you believe falsehoods about God's nature (he hates you, he partakes in evil), you will continue to feel like an unlovable outsider looking in on all the loveable and "normal" people. I was told that the abuse I experienced was God's judgment for my sin. It's no wonder some people hide from, hate, or are indifferent toward him.

Destructive passivity comes from plain old abandonment too. I pretty much raised myself—set my own curfews and prepared my own (not exactly balanced) meals. Whether I did homework or not was up to me. No one checked. No one asked questions. I went to parties on weekdays in junior high and high school. It didn't matter. I didn't think that I mattered.

I know what it's like to feel condemned to live another day, to not want to live another day, but feel you must because you wake up and find that fate still has you breathing. I took stupid risks with my body, which made sense because I didn't affirm its value. And all the while I gave the world that Nice Guy smile.

> **Abandonment deals a young boy's heart one of the deepest wounds imaginable; he will most likely come to believe he is unworthy to receive love and affection.**

Abandonment deals a young boy's heart one of the deepest wounds imaginable; he will most likely come to believe he is unworthy to receive love and affection. As a result, an adult Nice Guy spends much of his life salving this wound, often through the consumption of women, both emotionally and sexually. However, since Nice Guys don't possess what women really want and need, such as masculine support, strong protection, and emotional passion, they are destined to lose at love.

My mother feared the outside world and grew increasingly cloistered. She had a driver's license but never drove. She wouldn't walk around the block, saying that dogs might attack her, though such a thing had never happened to her as an adult. She had limited contact, yet had no shortage of opinions about how the world should operate. Fear and anxiety owned her, amping her up and wearing her out. She wore down those around her, and she passed these thoughts to me through the umbilicus of modeling.

Eventually, as I grew larger and taller, her abuse receded. Most abusive people are gifted at sticking their finger in the air, sensing changes, walking lines. Though they appear bold, they are cowards, because they usually attack only when assured of victory. Mess with their chances of success, and they often wither. It's the truly brave that continue regardless.

I remember the last time she tried, when I was about fourteen. She got me with a cheap right hook while standing in the dining room.

Her flabby tricep waddled. I was surprised by her lack of strength and her inability to muster that primal fury she once unleashed so effectively. Anger, as well as love, tends to cool with age.

I laughed at her.

"What are you doing?" I said, smiling. I could have, if I willed, crushed her with one hand, one blow. I looked down at her with the kind of pity you give an old lioness caged at a zoo.

That mystifying moment created an unofficial treaty: She would keep her hands and her words off of me. I made this easy for her, because I reduced her presence in my life. I called a lot of my own shots, even back then, and I sought her opinion less and less. I would eventually come to never seek it.

Life got much better thereafter. The dark days of junior high (I called them my gray years) broke out into the brighter skies of high school. I spent most of my teen years with good friends. I moved out when I was eighteen.

Her love became more apparent to me after that armistice. She became an advocate and a cheerleader. I can see now that she wanted to be closer and that those years of madness weren't about me. She was overwhelmed when I was younger, and she remained troubled for as long as I knew her. I tried to honor her the way a son should, and I kept her away as well. She could still unleash amazing disrespect and anger. She was incapable of apology, and I still don't know why; sincere apology may have paved the way for a better life for both of us.

She cried the day I moved away for good—it was the only time I could remember her crying at the thought of losing me. It spun my head: *All these years together,* I thought, *and you show me this side of you now?!* She told me later, a few years before she died, that the only time she saw her father cry for the loss of her was when she was leaving Ireland with my father on their honeymoon, to live in Canada. "Why did he wait so long to show me how he felt?" she mused. "That's a horrible thing, isn't it, to wait till you won't see the person again to show how you really feel."

Strange, not funny, how history repeats itself and how often it revolves around irony.

I loved her and she loved me. The abuse didn't mean her love wasn't real. Abuse made love harder to see, harder to believe, harder to trust. We grew closer the months before I stood by her deathbed, enduring that horrible death rattle, weeping.

THE FRUIT OF MISTREATMENT

How much cleaner and easier life would be if a strained relationship and a troubled soul could be set right when abuse stops and something better begins. Outside of feel-good movies, though, that's not how life works. The foundation of my thinking had been set, regardless of what rested upon it.

I'm not a robot and neither are you. Humans will react aversely to unjust treatment, especially at such a tender age, because that's how God made us, to feel. The question is, how?

Albert Einstein posed a fundamental question for which we need to muster much candor and wait some time before we answer: "Is the world a friendly place?" How could I answer but no, that it was something to be feared and avoided? So I learned how to hide my true feelings, avoid attention, and rarely confront. I had a Ph.D. in Passivity before I left elementary school.

Abuse rewires a kid's mind, much like a hacker gets into the good code of a program and rewrites it; the kid thinks he's defective and inferior to his fellow kid. And this is where a lot of Christians, especially preachers, make big mistakes. They say, "Hey, what's wrong with feeling guilt and conviction because of sin?" The answer is, nothing at all. That kind of guilt will help save your soul. But this isn't guilt I'm talking about.

Abused people believe that something is deeply wrong with them, not because they are *sinners,* but because they are *defective.* They become ashamed of themselves as humans, not because they fail, but because they exist. Accordingly, *troubled Nice Guys must learn to understand the difference between guilt and shame.*

> **Abused people believe that something is deeply wrong with them, not because they are *sinners,* but because they are *defective.* They become ashamed of themselves as humans, not because they fail, but because they exist.**

Guilt is not destructive to a person, because it's a response to what he does, and because something can be done about it. We can acknowledge our wrongdoing, change our behavior, and experience forgiveness.

Shame, however, goes beyond the understanding that "I did wrong things" to "I am worthless through and through." This is an anti-biblical view of creation, a lie that, when believed, robs you of how you perceive your own value.

Furthermore, if you aren't careful, you will become highly susceptible to people and organizations that use shame to control you. My friend Patrick Doyle, a counselor, warns such people that they have "shame Velcro®" all over them, and are prone to seek out people and groups that use it to their advantage. This is why *people with troubled pasts should avoid churches that make them feel ashamed for being human.*

A sense of who you are gets lost when you undergo such traumatic injustice as a kid. You have no real compass to find your way back to who you really are and to fight the lies that attack you. Everyone else, it seems, has the power and right to mold you. Everyone but you.

Abused children harbor a pervasive sense that they are inferior sub-species, children of a lesser god. They are unable to say to others, as Job did, "I am not inferior to you" (Job 12:3; 13:2). They are unable to state what Paul made clear to the Corinthians, that he did not see himself as inferior to other apostles, whom some referred to as "super-apostles" (2 Corinthians 11:5). When you believe you are inferior, you invite fear into the deepest recesses of your heart and become a sitting duck for destructive manipulation throughout the rest of your life.

So let's be clear here: Christian Nice Guys with this background are still sinners. It's not that because they had a tough childhood their sin isn't as vile as anyone else's. It should be clear, though, why they drag more baggage through life.

Feelings of worthlessness condemn CNGs to believe their lives won't and shouldn't amount to much, that they aren't wonderfully made by God (Psalm 139:14), and that they aren't his beloved creation, having been crowned with his glory and honor (8:5). In fact, living as if they are special to God seems *wrong;* they mistake their self-rejecting beliefs for God's thoughts toward them.

It's easy to see why Nice Guys truly believe God is out to get them. Grace remains alien because they think God doesn't stop at hating their sin—he hates *them* as well. As a result, they attack themselves and are quick to judge themselves by harsh, unbiblical standards. They bear false witness *against themselves.* When this rash of falsehoods is combined with radical feminist "shame rhetoric" and the church's low view of true masculinity, we discover why such men think they have nowhere to turn.

The far-reaching repercussions of this condition are seen in the lives of fearful and anxious people who, when perceiving themselves to be at conflict with their world, are prone to believe they are always at fault. This in turn makes them even more vulnerable to more shame and, as shown later, to the hidden agendas of others. Ultimately, if they remain in this state, genuine love is set, and kept, at arm's length.

PROBLEMS WITH TRUE LOVE

Repeated experiences of shame and self-hatred lead Nice Guys in general to terrorize their own lives. Perhaps the worst damage comes from their inability to love deeply, which is the greatest commandment. By default, in response to the biblical exhortation to love others as you love yourself, CNGs produce a shoddy love. The reason is this: *Love and fear cannot coexist. Where one exists, the other is banished.*

Nice Guys can't love well because they have too many guards up. Most of the time they are emotionally numb. At their best, they can achieve *philia*, a kind of love (from a Greek term) that means they're really fond of someone. And, because they're red-blooded guys (i.e., male humans), *erôs*, sexual wanting, often comes much more easily. (More accurately, their desire for sex is strong, but, true to form, their ability to experience satisfying sex and share real intimacy is limited.) It's *agapé*—deep and abiding love, that makes self-sacrifice possible, the love that leads to big dreams—that they can't achieve. They lack a heart of passion that carries out those dreams for God.

> **Love and fear cannot coexist. Where one exists, the other is banished.**

Their hearts aren't ready, because they've been subdued by fear and its barnacle-like growths. A Nice Guy won't ask that girl or that woman to dance, even when a part of him longs for her. He won't ask for a raise when it's deserved. He won't stand up to abusive people. He leaves his life open to attacks that others would never tolerate, Christian or not.

When CNGs read the last chapter of John, they may ache somewhere within their hidden self, since Peter's problem is their problem too. Twice Jesus asks Peter if he has *agapé* for him ("Do you truly love me?"), and twice Peter answers with *philia*: "You know that I love you." This is the best a Nice Guy can do because his heart is like a rare steak: warm on the outside, cool on the inside. To paraphrase, Jesus says, a third time, "Well, do you even feel *philia*, then?" Jesus knows man's timid heart, yet notice how he gets to the heart of the matter without destroying Peter through shaming words; he seeks to rebuild and restore.

Jesus embraced both of his inner "sides," gentle and tough. It's possible that Peter was ashamed to express genuine love for another man—*shame haunts Nice Guys.* It's also possible that he was too shy to reveal his heart to another, a life-strangling restriction that the truly masculine Jesus did not share.

I have felt *philia* for most of my life. When you're merely a *philia* man, you know on some level that you're missing out and it haunts you, usually at night as you stare out a dark window, watch your kids sleep, or strain to see the profile of your wife's face and wonder why you won't share your heart with her. Merely accepting your life, God, and others isn't enough to motivate you. You fall short, you "miss the mark," which is the definition of *hamartia,* one of the Greek words (taken from archery) from which we get the term *sin.*

Many CNGs are familiar with this concept, but haven't thought much about it; if they did, they'd be on the road to a greater life. *Hamartia* applies when we're aiming in the right direction, but our perception and abilities are somehow off; while this can give them hope with regard to their intentions, *Nice Guys need help, and there's no shame in admitting it.* I know so well how *philia* misses the best God offers. Today I know the dream-building life-breath of *agapé;* though I still guard against certain behaviors, the Nice Guy fallacy is gone.

OUR LIFE MOTTO

In response to life handing them such drawbacks at such young ages, CNGs form a naïve philosophy of life: "If I live small, my troubles will be few." This fearful motto haunts men into adulthood, causing them to play safe and killing spiritual growth, mind potential, and a heart energized by adventure and significance. NFL Hall of Fame quarterback Fran Tarkenton observed, "Fear causes people to draw back from situations; it brings on mediocrity; it dulls creativity; it sets one up to be a loser in life." Anxiety weighs our hearts down (Proverbs 12:25) and chokes God's healing word (Mark 4:19). Fear is a snare (Proverbs 29:25). God takes no pleasure in men who shrink back (Hebrews 10:38).

Regardless of whether they were abused, abandoned, neglected, shamed, the object of hyper-concern, or received similar sorrows, Christian Nice Guys believe, *This world is a dangerous place, God must be against me, and the key to making it through is to just keep my head down to avoid attention and* [shudder] *conflict.*

> **Nice Guys form a naïve philosophy of life: "If I live small, my troubles will be few."**

Though as an adult this tremulous mindset was often mysterious and haunting to me, it sometimes showed itself in flashes of clarity. I remember taking a shower as a married family man and hearing steps coming toward me down the hall. I tensed up. I thought someone was going to come into the bathroom and hit me, though such a thing had never happened to me in my home (and wasn't going to happen). Still, the fear was there, and because I did not ponder the situation further, and because I did not examine and address that fear, my life missed a huge opportunity for growth. Days passed one by one, bills demanded payment, tasks needed to be completed, and this potential insight languished inside me for lack of care and courage.

I know, as Chuck Swindoll points out, that comparisons are often odious, yet sometimes they are also helpful. For example, I used to observe men who went through a life similar to mine, and I saw that it didn't appear to be as hard for them. They possessed what seemed an innate confidence, a certain knowledge that they could handle whatever would come their way. They were emotionally more honest than I was. They didn't feel the same need to hide and to please.

Then I looked at myself. My emotional life was gummed up, and I didn't like it. Either I couldn't feel life the way I wanted to, or I wouldn't let myself—I didn't know which. I was like my first truck, a Chevy LUV: Yeah, it got me around town, but because the engine overheated, it worked a lot harder than it had to, and I would never take it on a long trip.

I was out of tune as well. Odd how we guys will tolerate an out-of-tune life while spending an entire weekend and large sums of money on an out-of-tune car. We don't want to undergo the frustration and embarrassment of having our vehicle give out on us, yet it's our cold heart that leaves us on the side of life's road. It's no coincidence that Nice Guys aren't successful in truly loving God and others.

I expended huge amounts of will. I can't tell you how many times I prayed that the Holy Spirit would come upon me afresh and *change* me. I saw men living larger, more dynamic lives, unafraid of passion. Their emotions propelled them, infusing their personas with color, levity, and power. I wanted that and was willing to undergo the struggle to get it.

My goal wasn't to become a SNAG (Sensitive New Age Guy), weepy and predictable, wearing my emotions on my sleeve and thinking the world was one long *kumbaya* moment. I didn't want to emote all the time, but man, what about showing emotions even when it just made sense? Like when my children were born. Like at a funeral for someone I loved, or at a celebration when I wanted to make a toast to someone special. Like at a movie, where a well-crafted storyline touches upon age-old sorrows; your head knows this is life, and it hurts, but your heart won't go there because you just don't cry—as in early life, crying will somehow get you into trouble.

This was my constipated existence, and it bothered me. Something was missing, and I worried I was also putting a similar heartless void in my children. I needed a change; I had reached the critical moment where I realized it would be a sin for me if I didn't. In choosing to begin seeing a counselor, I sought wisdom higher than my own.

I once attended a church where the pastor had an idyllic childhood. He spoke glowingly about how he'd never heard either his father or his mother yell. Physical violence was alien. Regardless, they did a great job of fortifying his young psyche, because he was among the most confident people I've ever met, and he had an ego to go along with it. I used to joke that it wasn't too big—just the size of St. Louis.

He criticized people who reached out for help with their troubled childhoods, and he denounced organizations like Focus on the Family that encourage such help. He thought all counseling, at least all counseling that was more than giving people chapters and verses from the Bible to read, was wrong in that it kept people from leaning solely on Christ. This was like saying you shouldn't go to an oncologist when you discover you have cancer. Even though that's exactly what some people do, *those* people are poor stewards of their body. After they die, do we really think their children are left with an example of living faith? (So goes the reasoning.)

This popular pastor was a man who knew grief as an adult, so he felt qualified to opine about the entire world of grief, failing to distinguish that pain as a child is far more fundamental than pain as an adult. He wasn't qualified, and when I said so, it was not well received.

He and others in the same misguided camp would do well to consider what C. S. Lewis wrote about professional help in no less than *Mere Christianity*, one of the most insightful books ever:

> Psychoanalysis itself, apart from all the philosophical additions that Freud and others have made to it, is not in the least contradictory to Christianity. . . . [There are irrational fears] which no amount of moral effort can do anything about . . . [and] bad psychological material is not a sin but a disease. It does not need to be repented of, but to be cured.

Humans, Lewis wrote, judge one another by external actions, which can be deceivingly simple.

> God judges them by their moral choices. . . . [So when an emotionally troubled person] who has a pathological horror of cats forces himself to pick up a cat for some good reason, it is quite possible that in God's eyes he has shown more courage than a healthy man. . . . Some of us who seem quite nice people may, in fact, have made so little use of a good heredity and a good upbringing that we're really worse than those whom we regard as fiends.

That is why Christians are told not to judge. We see only the results which a man's choices make out of his raw material. But God does not judge him on the raw material at all, but on what he has done with it.

Upon death,

All sorts of nice things, which we thought our own, but which were really due to a good digestion, will fall off some of us: all sorts of nasty things which were due to complexes or bad health will fall off others. We shall then, for the first time, see everyone as he really was. There will be surprises.

I'm hoping for a front-row seat.

I've experienced sorrow as a child and as an adult. I can't even begin to imagine what life would be like in a home where no one ever yelled or hit—a kind of Mayberry I'm glad some people get to experience. You are blessed among men if you're one of them, and I hope you don't squander this blessing by looking down your nose on those who struggle with the perplexing fallout of childhood trouble.

People like Hank, a beloved man in his sixties who came to KDOV radio station, where I was program director, to give his testimony. Hank was a local celebrity and politician. Live on the air, he shared how his mother didn't hold him when he was a little boy, which was a parenting trend at the time; she rarely showed him affection, believing that such displays somehow ruined children.

I wish more people could see what happens during commercial breaks, when the real stories unfold. Hank, accustomed to the many arrows of politics, bent his head forward, pinched the bridge of his nose, and wept. Hank was no wimp—he was stoic and brave in the face of opposition. Hank wasn't a man who never grew up or didn't know how to rightly share his emotions. Hank had a fundamental void inside, and even though it was one that God helped him handle, the ache, the lack, was inescapable, the rejection unavoidable for the human heart. We were created with the capacity for sorrow, and given the state of this world, sorrow we will feel.

Many Christian men and women who have not undergone the struggles I've described talk loosely about things they don't understand, and their ignorance often makes them dangerous bigots. If you are any part of this camp, do your brothers and sisters a favor: Be quiet. Timid Christian Nice Guys need our help, not our disapproval. We damage them further by denying their painful afflictions and refusing to comprehend how it undercuts them. Remind them of what the Roman poet Ovid wrote: "Be patient and tough; some day this pain will be useful to you."

The unfortunately common church response to weak Christian men is to throw words at them. It does no good to tell a CNG to "be a man," to "just get over it," to "pray more." We wouldn't be so callous with a woman's pain, but we are with a man's.

Though prayer is vital, it's *not* the fundamental issue facing Christian Nice Guys. Here's the foundational question they need to answer: *Can my pain be transformed into something grand, like a greater ability to love, to protect, and to utilize a righteous kind of power?*

The first part of the answer to this is, yes, God gave you a more powerful nature. He did not give you your current timid spirit (2 Timothy 1:7). *That* spirit came from this world, from a childhood that taught you to live small and/or from a culture (and subculture) that fails to understand masculinity.

We'll have to wrestle with other portions of our lives to partake in the Good Guy Rebellion; love and marriage is the subject of the next chapter. Like I said earlier, this work is a form of rebellion that treads on delicate ground. Bob Seger, sage of men's souls, sang that once a man obtains a woman's affections, watch out: Heaven opens up situations where "angels fear to tread."

To think otherwise is to be naïve.

HOW BEING "NICE" RUINS LOVE AND MARRIAGE

"Women aren't attracted to you. You put out that *nice guy* vibe."

—CARRIE TO HER HUSBAND, DOUG, ON *KING OF QUEENS*

Contrary to the popular saying, most Nice Guys don't finish last; it might be better if they did, so they'd need to make changes earlier. But they sure don't finish first, either. They finish somewhere in the frustrated middle, somewhere around room temperature. CNGs are lukewarm males, whose talents go unused and whose desires are unmet. Remember what Jesus said about the lukewarm? Today, dissatisfaction and disillusionment leak out of them in the form of visiting porn sites, drinking too much, obsessing over hobbies . . . the list goes on, and nothing on it leads to happy relationships.

One of life's saddest paradoxes is that you will sometimes dread what you work the hardest to obtain. This is true for women who, with the aid of pop teaching and pop culture, expect men always to be sweet and compliant, only later finding these same men boring and unattractive. Ultimately, women aren't drawn to or captivated by men who are all sweet pickle and no jalapeño. Acting nice all the time leads to problems across the board, none more painful for Christian Nice Guys than in love and marriage. Statistically, many of them are headed for divorce.

MARRIAGE WOES FOR THE CNG

When I brought the fear-based passivity of my youth into my young marriage and combined it with the false ideal of "gentle Jesus, meek and mild," fireworks exploded. But I'm fortunate. I got a handle on my farcical niceness before I fatally wounded my one and only union, now of fifteen years.

Like many spouses of CNGs, my wife, Sandy, could easily teach assertiveness training courses. Her personality contains what our Hawaiian friends call *Kolohe,* which means "rascal." Sandy's alive, vibrant, and vivacious, especially in social settings. So she couldn't comprehend why I'd get nervous about common situations like parties.

"Why don't you want to go?" she'd ask, confused and frustrated.

"I'd rather read," I'd say, which was partly true, but also a cop-out. I really didn't want to face potential conflict, even though I hadn't done or said anything that would warrant meaningful criticism. Crowds just scared me, not that I would admit it. (Talk about an unattractive and conflicted stick-in-the-mud.)

Sandy also loves to entertain—she's full of life when she's doing it, and she's rarely more beautiful than during these evenings. But the thought of guests used to terrify me. *What if the conversation stalls? What will I say? What if dinner gets delayed? What will I do then?* I was stuck in the no-win world of *What If* thinking instead of the healthy *So What?* approach. One thing I did know: If she likes entertaining this much, I'd better get on board or forget being really close with her, because intimate couples share their bliss. My desire for a strong and intimate marriage motivated me to face my fears.

Providing for my family was tough as well. I was no match for co-workers and bosses who knew they could bowl me over: They laid all sorts of blame and responsibility in my cubicle that fell completely outside my job description. But I followed my church's advice to turn the cheek to all wrongdoing, and as I endured this treatment my paycheck eventually suffered.

In addition, I don't want to remember what we now joke about as the Sex Wars. Because I was scared to be direct with my sexual desires (remember, when we were kids, Nice Guys got in big trouble for having normal wants), I took the covert route.

I thought I was a smooth operator. I'd pat her on the rear or rub her back or stroke her thick dark hair, usually in the kitchen at evening time. This was how I'd form an unofficial pact: I'll show you affection, you throw some my way, baby. When she didn't, I'd blow up (or pout) because she didn't fulfill her end of our agreement—an agreement she'd never made.

In the Christian Nice Guy's marriage, all this happens without it being talked about. It simmers just below the surface, where CNGs want it—we *are* a manipulative lot. But the silent pressure and the covert expectations are real. My wife says she felt them, even though she couldn't put her finger on them: "Looking back, I walked on eggshells, but I didn't know it. I knew something was wrong, but I couldn't name it. It didn't have a name then."

Because I dreaded conflict, I would tell one person (say, my mother) what she wanted to hear, then tell another (say, my frustrated wife) something different. Such a scenario may make for a great sitcom, but it's not funny in real life. There's a word for this behavior: Lying. Smell the brewing of marital conflict.

I've talked with self-described Christian Nice Guys across the country who have similar stories. Most don't want to be identified, so I've changed their names, but their experiences are accurate. One, employed in Christian publishing, read my writing about this problem and said, "That's me. That's what happened to my marriage. This is why I'm divorced." He flashed me a fake smile to cover his pain and throw me off his path. He didn't seem to have much interest in getting to the root of the problem. He just wanted it to go away. *He* just wanted to go away.

Says Tim, a struggling CNG from Alabama: "The church encourages Christian men to be passive, and this leads to broken relationships and opportunities. Christians are taught that it's sinful to tell others what one really thinks and feels. This is damaging because people are naturally expressive."

INCORRECT MEANINGS OF "SACRIFICE"

In men's groups, I've seen guys break down and cry when realizing the chasm between what the church has told them to be and who they are as made by God. They feel right when they provide for and support their families—they say it's a great feeling, unlike any other, packed with meaning and purpose. However, they have been convinced that this means if they're being like Jesus—if they're being servants—then they will have no needs or requirements or expectations of their own.

> **No man in his right mind gets married solely to serve; he has wishes, needs, and desires as well.**

This is *not* true servanthood. Even so, no man in his right mind gets married solely to serve; he has wishes, needs, and desires as well. The church has told him this is selfish and sinful; psychologically unhealthy women latch on to this sweet-sounding nonsense, using it against their husbands, and Christian Nice Guys hide behind it also. There is a part of them that *doesn't* think they should require or ask for anything. But the God-given part, the true man, knows he has dignity, including inherent needs and desires. Men long to be respected by their wife or girlfriend yet are told that such longing is un-Christian; again, *those who don't require respect don't receive it.* Contradictions everywhere mean the internal frustrations build, and so do the tears of the men still alive enough to shed them; for the ones who aren't, if they don't acknowledge and face the conflict, the inner battle works them over, and they become destined to either explode or implode.

Christian men are told to "love your wives, just as Christ loved the church and gave himself up for her" (Ephesians 5:25). So what does this sacrifice entail, and how literal is the admonishment?

We saw earlier that love incorporates many actions and thoughts spanning the emotional, volitional, and behavioral spectrum. Love can be gentle, tough, and confrontational (Proverbs 27:5–6). The Bible even goes so far as to say, "Let a righteous man strike me—it is a kindness; let him rebuke me—it is oil on my head" (Psalm 141:5).

When you strip away the veneer of spiritual-sounding "virtues," Christian Nice Guys have been encouraged to be doormats for their wives. This is not loving sacrifice, and it is not attractive. Why? Because it violates an ironclad law of human nature: We don't respect passive people any more than we like aggressive people. *The goal is to become assertive.* (More on that later.)

Some women are more than happy to marry a weak man, because they can control him; in fact, they have no interest in any other kind. But such women are self-destructive: "Wait until she needs a real man during a time of crisis," Dr. Laura told me. "She'll want a man with backbone then, and he won't be found."

Mentally balanced wives don't respect passivity. A passive husband is an unreliable husband, and this makes his wife anxious, because she knows it will leave her and the children open to difficulties that threaten the family. Most women won't just sit there and let such damage happen; they will do something. One choice a wife can make is to become overtly

> • **We don't respect passive people any more than we like aggressive people. *The goal is to become assertive.***

critical and even ridiculing—and some do—but this will never bring about the results she truly needs. A much better (and much more difficult) choice is to help her husband see what fear and anxiety are doing to his life.

I had a Christian roommate who blew my mind regarding marriage. He was prone to hyper-spiritual ideas, and so a popular interpretation of Ephesians 5:25 was right up his alley. He said that if he got married, he would have to sell everything that brought him pleasure and relaxation; his new life would have to revolve around his wife, for whom he was required to sacrifice his entire being. In his mind, that was how he would live up to every word of Scripture. But let's look at where this approach would lead.

Imagine how smothered his wife would feel; she'd likely think, *He must believe I'm an imbecile, that I can't do anything on my own.* She wouldn't feel like a treasure. She'd feel pitied. She'd feel trapped. The wine of her love would become a water of obligation; only what's freely given is a blessing to the giver and to the receiver.

What about him? Do we really think women respect men who have no life of their own, who live only for another person? We know that characterless people don't garner respect, yet for some reason we think this magically changes when two believers marry. Spiritualized spin-doctoring is *not* going to change who we are.

What's being done to Christian men today is similar to what was done to Christian women years ago, when they were told, "Just submit, and your marriage will get better." Now we're telling men, "Sacrifice your identity for your wife, and your marriage will be strong." Exactly what a culture obsessed with quick fixes wants to hear, but life doesn't work that way.

We should also keep in mind that Paul is making an analogy in Ephesians, and, as Logic 101 demonstrates, all analogies are incomplete. If this analogy *were* complete, we husbands would blasphemously think we were Christ and our wives the church. Paul is saying we must sacrifice for our wives and our families on the whole; our soul feels right when we do, and we should know that we are choosing selfishness if we do not. The future of the Nice Guy's marriage depends on interpreting this teaching as it was intended to be understood, which includes the need for a baseline of respect.

Unconditional love is beautiful and imperative when dealing with small children. The same type of unconditional love toward an adult—without requiring respect—is foolish and damaging. That my wife and I demand respect from each other has kept our marriage from some tremendous pitfalls. Respect is a mirror that can compel a person to face issues in his or her life that might otherwise be completely avoided and thereby fester and build beneath the surface.

THE SOUND OF DIVORCE PAPERS RUSTLING

When CNGs scrub themselves of strength that once made their wives and children feel secure, alive, and respectful, it's a matter of time before subtle discontent and contempt set in, sometimes leading to divorce. Writes one wife: "My husband has no backbone, and it's hard to respect him. If I'm honest, I don't respect him. He's so non-confrontational, and it has gotten me and my family into more and more problems." As it stands, how long do you think that marriage is going to last?

I asked my wife and her friend (a preacher's daughter) why their mutual friend left her husband, and it was one of those moments when people just state the facts without running them through churchy filters. I'm still floored by their response, nearly in unison: "Because he was too nice."

This church elder did what the church told him to do: exorcise himself of uniqueness and give, give, and give some more, expecting little if anything in return. He required no respect, so his wife lost her respect for him; the church's guidance reduced him to a vanilla identity and then had the gall to blame him for the divorce.

Want more evidence that your marriage is in danger when you follow the Nice Guy script? The fact that two-thirds of all divorces involving couples with children are initiated by wives should motivate CNGs toward change. Contrary to feminist lore, most women don't divorce their husbands due to abuse (only about 6 percent), but because of a general lack of closeness or of "not feeling loved and appreciated" (from S. L. Braver and D. O'Connell, *Divorced Dads: Shattering the Myths*, 1988).

Again, Christian Nice Guys, void (or nearly void) of discernible masculine energy and vitality, specialize in a lack of closeness and an inability to deeply love another—they're sitting ducks for relational catastrophe.

Many Nice Guys marry vivacious women who eventually grow tired of trying to coax life out of a low-voltage husband. Worse, CNGs sometimes suppress their spouse's outgoing personality, a kiss of death for any marriage. Governed by fear rather than by love, Nice Guys drain their wives of strength and ability; by contrast, men who live according to love instead of fear vitalize their wives and encourage them to explore and develop their gifts.

The church sometimes gives us an incomplete understanding of commitment, making matters worse; we're told that being committed is synonymous with just hanging in there. *That's* actually closer to endurance. Commitment is better understood as applying yourself to a task or goal. It includes investment, not merely stamina. Commitment is proactive, not stoically reactive to a lousy situation. (Proactivity also serves as radiation treatment to CNG cancer. More on this later.)

PASSION IS NOT A PROBLEM

Why does contemporary Christianity encourage mild living, when Jesus showed more (not less) passion than anyone else around him? Alfred Lord Tennyson noted that "the happiness of a man in this life does not consist in the absence but in the mastery of his passions." C. S. Lewis wrote:

> **Why does contemporary Christianity encourage mild living, when Jesus showed more (not less) passion than anyone else around him?**

> It would seem that our Lord finds our desires not too strong, but too weak. We are half-hearted creatures, fooling about with drink and sex and ambition when infinite joy is offered us, like an ignorant child who wants to go on making mud pies in a slum because he cannot imagine what is meant by the offer of a holiday at the sea. We are far too easily pleased. (*The Weight of Glory*, 3–4)

The church tells Christian men to lead, but then strips them of the emotional power to do so by warning them to be "moderate in all things" and keeping them fearful about upsetting their wives. Men are frequently treated like outsiders in cowboy movies: Check your gun at the saloon door. Look at how Lewis addressed this:

> All the time—such is the tragi-comedy of our situation—we continue to clamor for those very qualities we are rendering impossible. You can hardly open a periodical without coming across the statement that what our civilization needs is more "drive," or dynamism, or self-sacrifice, or "creativity." In a sort of ghastly simplicity we remove the organ and demand the function. We make men without chests and expect of them virtue and enterprise. We laugh at honor and are shocked to find traitors in our midst. We castrate and bid the geldings be fruitful. (*The Abolition of Man*)

Thank God that *Jesus* wasn't moderate in all things.

We caution against passion because it can lead to destruction. True, it can. But that's like saying we shouldn't drive cars because someone might drive too fast. What about harnessing that power, the way most of us have learned to do with vehicles? Passion, emotional energy, bravery, guided by the Holy Spirit, leads to redeemed and enhanced marriages. It's a motor that moves you toward healthy life and away from divorce and its related destruction. What better reason do you need to begin this change *today*?

BEING NICE KEEPS YOU SINGLE

The church's thoughts on dating aren't usually clear or well articulated, but often it seems that because this cultural ritual is fraught with potential difficulties, the church holds that Christians are better off just avoiding it. Avoidance by default, not moving for fear of failing, hiding for fear of being seen—in most areas of life, this is what I've come to expect from the church (except, of course, in regard to food that's bad for us).

One insightful single CNG told me, "I'm trying to break away from the societal influences that have caused many men to become laid back rather than bold, reserved rather than outgoing and honest." I told him that unfortunately one of these "influences" is the church. But many single Christian men know that the Nice Guy route isn't working, while also not having a clue as to why. Some truly believe that their pleasant passivity is God-ordained, so frequently they simply assume there's something intrinsically wrong with *women.*

Single women have their own insights that are more on target. One who works for a large Christian publishing house told me, "My single Christian girlfriends and I say that the best man to date has only been in the church for two years. This way he still has some masculinity left." *How* she said it was funny. *What* she said should push us to our knees and ignite righteous indignation.

Her shocking observation harkened my mind back to when I was a single CNG listening to another sermon designed to make me a swell guy. The popular pastor ended his message about "biblical" marriage with an illustration about three chauffeurs. Two wanted to show their driving prowess, so they drove close to the edges of a winding road to showcase their abilities and bravery. The third played by all the rules. He stayed away from the edges (danger, risk, conflict) and played it safe, just as a CNG should.

His admonishment was clear: *Play life safe, you guys—don't rock any boats at home.* I was single, love-hungry, floating in a sea of earnest and passive young men. Putting such a message in front of us was like shoving a stiff drink in front of a struggling alcoholic; this charismatic and powerful speaker put damaging temptation smack-dab in my face and said it was from God. Truthfully, it flies in the face of Scripture: "We who are strong ought to bear with the failings of the weak" (Romans 15:1). For some men, safety is a hiding place for sinful faithlessness.

WHY MASCULINE MEN ARE "JERKS"

When one CNG asked how he could make women like him more and the "jerks" out there less, I replied, "The 'jerks,' as you say, possess a power that you don't have. Women aren't attracted to people who don't show much personality." He didn't like hearing this any more than I enjoyed saying it; like many of us, he grew up in a church culture that falsely equated mildness with virtue. Here's what we must acknowledge: The Nice Guy's mission, his personal goal, is not to be an agent of redemption, but to leave a likable impression. This does *not* emulate or honor Jesus.

Bill's friend says Bill is biblically literate, culturally relevant, doctrinally sound, verbally articulate, physically fit, and remarkably considerate. "Yet [Bill] doesn't have much luck in the dating arena. He is the quintessential 'nice guy.'" He thought it would be a good idea for me to talk with Bill, so I did.

> **The Nice Guy's mission, his personal goal, is not to be an agent of redemption, but to leave a likable impression. This does *not* emulate or honor Jesus.**

Bill grew up in a legalistic church where the "pastor's emotionless lifestyle" permeated the entire congregation. Bill is forty-six and has never been married, but wants to be. *Really* wants to be: "I'm immature in developing relationships. I'm passive, I avoid conflict, and I'm afraid of women. Single women are hard to talk to, so I like talking with married women. I guess I'm threatened by the possibility that I might have to take a chance with a single woman. It's no fun coming home alone every day."

Bill was engaged nine years ago, but he broke it off and hasn't had a girlfriend since. Though he often wonders why this is the case, he suspects it hasn't much to do with physical appearances: "My friend is fat and bald. He would probably agree that he's not really good-looking. But his wife is a babe. Looks aren't as important to women as they are to men."

When I suggest that women are attracted to men who have inner energy and their own will, Bill's not sure what to think. He's in what I call the Single Christian Nice Guy Funk: Even though a wealth of evidence points directly to the true problem, he doesn't see it or doesn't want to see it.

Because Christian men are encouraged to be compliant, malleable, and without relational requirements, they often lack the ethos and charisma that attract a woman's heart. Pete, a CNG from California, is coming to terms with how this message short-circuits his desire for intimacy: "I wanted a woman's approval so much that I would do anything for them. Women just don't respect this quality in a man."

That women aren't attracted to single CNGs is why Ken, the son of rigid Pentecostal parents, began to look at his issues: "I was too agreeable, and I focused too much of my attention on her. It really blew me away when I discovered that doesn't work." He learned later through a mutual friend that his ex-girlfriend wanted him to stand up to her, but given what he had heard and learned at church, he didn't feel he should.

I still remember one date where I stood up to a smart young woman's false accusation toward me. I analyzed it, exposed its inconsistencies, and then threw it back at her. I wasn't *always* a Nice Guy, and I figured then that I'd either ruined or improved the relationship. Her calculated and somewhat cold countenance thawed before my nervous eyes. Her eyes relaxed and invited me; my response clearly made me more attractive to her. I later found out that she threw this same statement at every young man she wanted to pursue. Those who had backbone and self-respect made it to the next cut. Those who didn't were gone.

Peter, a Christian magazine editor, shares his formative experience: "Growing up, I learned the right things to say, the things you were supposed to do, in church, like never get discouraged and always speak positively, even when situations were bad. The right thing to do was always to seek someone's approval, not rock the boat, and just be safe."

If he played in a tree house, for example, his mom would warn him to stay away from the edge. "Play life safe. That's the message I got from my mom and the church. The church also told me that if I was angry, then I was sinning. I was to keep it to myself. I wasn't supposed to have opinions either, so in college I suppressed what I thought, even though you're supposed to explore what you think in college so you can be educated."

His father was an alcoholic: "He got violent when he drank, and he'd call the next day asking for forgiveness. I learned pretty early that my mother's world was the right one and that my father's world was the wrong one."

Still, he couldn't help but be drawn to his father's more rugged life. "He tortured us in the outdoors. I loved it. I remember playing catch in a pool with a football when it was about forty degrees outside."

When Peter was bothered that he didn't have any girls on his arm in college, his friend, a Christian, but not a Nice Guy, set him straight: "[My friend] had long hair and was a great athlete. He was cool. I thought I was a dork, and there was no way I could get the girl of my dreams. He told me I was wrong, and that I shouldn't think that about myself. He told me I had a lot to give a woman. It was difficult to take the first step into confidence, but it was something I wanted enough to pursue."

The last I heard, Peter was engaged to a strong woman.

My son Garrett is named after a man who taught me writing, photography, jazz, poetry, theology, and how to think more clearly over steaming cups of straight espresso. "A man can do good at work and he can do good at home, but it's hard to do both" was one of his more haunting statements that still sticks in my mind.

Garrett built a home out of trees that he cut and milled himself. It really was a tree house, about fourteen hundred square feet in a remote valley with no electricity. A founding elder of a local church, he spoke boldly about God and about the problems he saw in their congregation. He came to feel as though the church had cast him away, so he lived the life of a Christian exile, hanging outside the camp, waiting for the church to be able and willing to accept someone like him. Like other men in this book, he had fellowship with Christian brothers and sisters, but he felt alien to church culture.

At my home, three days before he died, Garrett played a delicate Bill Evans song by heart—"Turn Out the Stars." (Evans, one of my favorite jazz pianists, composed it during the three days between his father's death and when he was to play Carnegie Hall for the first time.) Garrett was riding his beloved motorcycle, coming back from a showing of his watercolors halfway across the state, when he missed a doe but hit its fawn on a back road around dusk. He died instantly.

Garrett's wife was beautiful—she looked like Sophia Loren. He wrote poetry about her, and some of it made me blush when he read the early drafts to me; unlike the other Christian men in my life, he talked about sex as if it were enjoyable, actually worth waiting for. After he died, Christian guys were lining up to date his widow (though they tried not to show it), and when I asked, "Has anyone asked you out?" she said, "They are all so nice. And boring. They can't come close to Garrett."

My dear brother had fire in his belly. He spoke truth like an Old Testament prophet. He could be hard and demanding. He threw photos at me. "Don't show me this [expletive] again," he growled when I brought pictures that repeated earlier mistakes.

I'll take one rugged Garrett to half the men in a given congregation today. I haven't met anyone like him in the church since. That hole has not been filled, and I doubt it will be.

Not requiring respect from others and having no true opinion is not the way to love. Christian Nice Guy: Stop trying to be a woman's best friend. Stop stripping yourself of the masculinity that draws her toward you. Most of the men who possess this energy aren't jerks; you possess the same power they have, but you wrongly think it's off-limits to you. Don't settle for being envious; find that energy, that power, that passion, then embrace it and apply it.

FEAR, OUR CONFIDENCE KILLER

Confidence is one of life's most attractive attributes, especially in a man. Fear, the emotional state that drives and owns Christian Nice Guys, is the lethal enemy of confidence.

My wife's respect for me grew once I got a handle on fear. And intimacy, which I'd wanted for years and played all sorts of games to get, finally flourished. Until CNGs address their fear, they will rarely if ever appear attractive to women, at least for very long.

Confident men are strong team members; with a confident man, a woman knows she has joined arms with an imperfect leader who doesn't have to manipulate or be nursed or be fixed. Sure, he licks his wounds, he complains sometimes, and he has a heart that feels life's heaviness, but fear and shame don't own him. He shows courage not by being a lone ranger, but by letting those closest to him actually be close, as Jesus did. He's not fearless, but he does fear less.

CNGs need to listen to time-honored insights on marriage instead of the trendy stuff we hear today, the messages that center on so-called secret formulas to success in love. The components of a strong and fulfilling marriage have been around for a long time.

During one Focus on the Family radio interview, Dr. James Dobson, Dr. Henry Cloud, and Dr. John Townsend discussed the problems that hinder men who want to marry but find that intimacy eludes them due to their Christian Nice Guy behavior.

The *best* way to pull another toward you, said Dr. Dobson, "is to express self-confidence, excitement with life, optimism, interest in many things, a certain independence, and a certain ability to go on unconnected with anybody for the rest of their life if that's what God requires."

This list of assertive attributes is nearly opposite of those possessed and expressed by CNGs. The *worst* way to pull someone toward you "is to convey right up front all of those needs and feelings and insecurities and attach them to the first possibility that comes along." This reminds me, Christian Nice Guys: Do not tell a woman that she's beautiful on the first date. Give it some time. You aren't required to say everything you think. Being wise as a serpent requires strategy; that probably somehow feels to you like lying, but it isn't—you need to get over it.

Dr. Cloud said that passive men are most unattractive to women: "They won't stand up for themselves," won't pursue their own interests, are "yes" men.

"Women want a man with a will of his own. They want a whole person," said Dr. Townsend. Emotionally injured men need to realize that "their injury is their responsibility to fix, which may require professional help. When we demand that someone else makes us whole, we will chase that person away." Such a man needs to become goal-oriented, become a risk taker, and become more assertive. (We'll later explore these important factors.)

Single CNGs who want to be married should also ignore the words of a former singles pastor of mine (and I've heard other pastors say the same thing); he said that any guy who attends a function for single Christians and is interested in finding a spouse is a "predator." His advice, rather, was solely to pray about the situation, and then God, he believed, would bring the woman of my dreams right into my arms via nuptial special delivery—I just needed to pray, then sit back and wait. This stationary approach to life was poisonous to me then and it's poisonous to the kind of man I'm fighting to help now.

Was I really what the dictionary says a predator is: one who "victimizes," "plunders," or "destroys"? I didn't know that. I thought I was a guy who wanted to marry another Christian, who had been told to do so, and who'd figured out that a good place to find such a person, when the time was right, was at church functions that had the highest concentration of such women. That wasn't the only reason I went, but it was one reason. Talk about belittling the heart of a guy.

I wish more people would have the guts to stand against the passivity that is choking the life out of Christian men. Chuck Swindoll writes, "It is absolutely imperative, men, that we fight our tendency to be passive in matters pertaining to the home. The passive husband continues to be one of the most common complaints I hear from troubled homes" (*Bricks That Build a Marriage*).

But when Christian men are told to pare vital emotional energy, not to require respect and thereby receive none (we don't follow people we don't respect), to rid themselves of distinguishing features that jettison masculinity, then what else can we expect? Our motto isn't "We're Christian Men. Hear Us Roar!" It's "We're Christian Men. Hear Us Bleat."

I still wonder why we think we have to put a smiley face on all of life

(Jesus didn't). I still wonder why we think that the absence of conflict is the greatest measure of marital harmony. Given our desire to sweep away life's innate difficulties and call them something else, I wonder what we evangelicals would do if it were up to us to decide which of the Bible's books are worthy of the scriptural canon. For instance, I don't think Job and Ecclesiastes would see the light of day—they don't deliver any 24/7 good vibration, the way most worship music is designed to do. (Side note: *Should* men really want to stand and emote for forty-five to sixty minutes at the beginning of a service? What about a mixture of music that touches both our hearts and our heads? There's no law that says it must be sentimental *all the time*.)

I also think Paul's letter to Philemon is too crafty for the canon. And I believe Song of Songs would end up in the fire; it's far too racy for (falsely) pious church people—they're much like those whom Jesus insulted—and it inspires passion, which terrifies many of us.

If you were to withhold the name of the book, and show the steamier passages of Song of Songs to the good church folk this week, some would likely throw it on the ground and call it the writing of a pervert. In so doing, they would discard the heart of men as well. That is the subject of the next chapter.

WE'RE MEN, NOT EUNUCHS

His head resting between my breasts—the head of my lover.

—SONG OF SONGS 1:13
(THE MESSAGE)

You are tall and supple, like the palm tree, and your full breasts are like sweet clusters of dates. I say "I'm going to climb that palm tree! I'm going to caress its fruit! Oh yes! Your breasts. . . ."

—SONG OF SONGS 7:8–9
(THE MESSAGE)

The Bible celebrates sex within the context of wedded bliss, but you wouldn't know it from a typical church service or an hour of Christian radio: Christendom has yet to shout it from the mountaintops with the same gusto it has the value of domesticity (that is, a female definition of domesticity). If the church wants to help create *real* domestic tranquility—and in the process draw more men to (and back to) church—it will make this fundamental issue its next battle cry. Nice Guys or otherwise, men *will* notice the church showing that it's serious about who they are, what they need, what they desire. But in order for this shift to take place, we need to do battle with a Sunday-morning force as powerful as the expectation for three-point sermons and weak coffee: *false piety*. We'll address false piety later in this chapter.

SURVEY SAYS: CHRISTIAN WOMEN HAPPY ... CHRISTIAN MEN NOT SO HAPPY

When surveyed, Christian women express higher levels of marital satisfaction than any other group, religious or not (Brad Wilcox interview in *Books and Culture*). No such study gives Christian men reason to celebrate, and an unwillingness to create emotional intimacy is among the heaviest complaints I receive from husbands about their wives. They lament that their wives don't even perceive sexual intimacy, which in its emotional union is far more than just sexual activity, as a key component in keeping a couple together; their wives behave as if intimacy is a hassle or an extracurricular activity. This problem is worse for the CNGs who have not yet developed the traits that women find attractive in the first place.

Many Christian wives have been brought up without an understanding of this essential issue. They went to the right schools, they have accurate theology, they attend church regularly, they're well-trained in the importance of raising happy children; yet they don't see the value of regular intimacy with their husbands. I'm amazed by how insufficiently women understand a man's heart and how poorly some wives treat it.

For most men, a desire for sex is as fundamental as a desire for food, and not only does something die inside a married man when this desire isn't met, something can also be perverted for lack of pure fulfillment. Sex isn't the only reason why some guys get married (at least it shouldn't be), but it's a biggie. As I've said on my talk show many times, if men, especially younger ones, say they aren't getting married to have sex, then chances are they're already having it.

> **I'm amazed by how insufficiently women understand a man's heart and how poorly some wives treat it.**

A Christian man struggles to maintain sexual purity in a culture that says he's crazy. (Once when I told co-workers that my wife and I waited till after marriage, they looked at me as if I'd just gotten off the shuttle from Pluto.) In a common scenario, an unmarried Christian man knows he could have sex with many women, but he withholds and endeavors to wait. He fights back temptation after temptation to please God and to give his future wife the gift of sexual purity. Then at last he marries and crosses the finish line, yet instead of fabulous banquets, he gets frozen dinners for years to come. Such men will tell you they feel robbed, resentful, victims of false advertising.

Women, sexual intimacy tells a man that you care about him and him only; it's how he feels special. It is to men what chocolate, diamonds, peaceful homes, and memorable vacations are to you. Sex is our *Lifetime Network,* our *Oprah.* Sex is the closest we get to being those screaming, insane girls at a Beatles concert. Our days, like yours, are often arduous; sex is where we feel that all of our sacrifice is worth it, appreciated, noticed. Sexual intimacy freely given somehow stabilizes our universe. It's our action to your words, our shelter from the storms of life; you are the safest harbor in which we'll ever make port. Sex is also the sharpest, most jagged knife in our back when it's not given or, worse, given without passion, focus, and interest. We can tell. Our pain is far more nuanced than you realize.

Attempting to ward off or at least cope with the hurt, Christian men try to joke about it. Here are just some of the names I've heard to describe unsatisfying sex: Check-her-pulse sex, did-I-detect life? sex, refund sex, mercy sex, pity sex, I'm-tired-so-hurry-up sex, 50%-off sex, 9-1-1 sex, undertaker sex, wouldn't-pass-lie-detector sex, jewelry sex, new-car sex (but rarely sex in the car), and bigger-home sex. *What we really want and need is There's-No-One-Like-You sex.* That's our physical and emotional Promised Land, and there are too few of us making camp there. We need your help!

I've heard a Christian man say to his wife, in front of a full dinner table, "I'll get you back someday" for rarely being "in the mood." It wasn't the merlot talking either. It was his spurned heart crying out sideways. Lifeless sex whispers or shouts the same horrible message to all of us: *insulting.*

Here's a somewhat famous letter, circulated among disgruntled husbands, that attempts to salve their pain with humor:

To My Loving Wife:

During the past year I have tried to make love to you 365 times. I have succeeded only thirty-six times, an average of once every ten days. The following is a list of the reasons why I did not succeed more often: it was too late, too early, too hot, or too cold. It would awaken the children, the company in the next room, or the neighbors whose windows were open. You were too full, or you had a headache, a backache, a toothache, or the giggles. You pretended to be asleep or were not in the mood. You had on your mudpack. You watched the late TV show; I watched the late TV show; the baby was crying.

During the times I did succeed, the activity was not entirely satisfactory for a variety of reasons. On six occasions you chewed gum the whole time; every so often you watched TV the whole time. Frequently you told me to hurry up and get it over with. A few times I tried to awaken you to tell you we were through; and one time I was afraid I had hurt you, for I felt you move.

Honey, it's no wonder I drink too much.

Your Loving Husband

Christian men are challenging why we don't see eye to eye on sex. Writes one *New Man* magazine reader from California: "I am sick of Christian magazines proposing that every sexual problem in marriage is the husband's fault. . . . [Your article about sex suggests] that if a husband is not sexually satisfied in marriage, it is probably because he has not properly honored his wife. At the risk of being politically incorrect, may I suggest that women in the church are not pulling their weight in marriage either? There is nothing that wounds a husband deeper than his wife's neglect. We men have a lot of work to do, but giving wives a carte blanche absolution for this is unrealistic and insulting. Men should know better."

There's that painful term again: *insulting.*

Why is this happening? In part, because of the church's response to this pivotal issue. Writes Phillip Yancey in *Reaching for the Invisible God:*

It should be obvious why the church so often falls on the side of repression, rather than celebration, of sexuality: No human longing is more powerful, more difficult to rein in. Sex has enough combustive force to incinerate conscience, vows, family commitments, religious devotion, and anything else in its path. How the church got its reputation as an enemy of sex is a long story, in some ways shameful and in some ways understandable.

The church's reluctance to embrace and rejoice in our sometimes incendiary sexual desire is understandable in regard to its presence within a culture that has lost its mind about the meaning and responsibility that comes along with it. Inarguably, however, ignoring, belittling, misrepresenting, and marginalizing sex also causes profound damage. It's time for the pendulum to swing back to the middle, back to a place of common sense for all and of mutual respect between men and women. Much simmering anger and fomenting rage will be skimmed off the top of gender relations when we do.

THE GRIP OF FALSE PIETY

False piety, a behavior that easily and quickly got under Jesus' skin, is at the heart of why the church won't embrace the legitimate sexual needs of husbands and, accordingly, encourage wives to take this area of their marriage more seriously.

"Piety" is religious devotion and reverence for God. "False piety" is to pretend, usually through lip service, that you believe something is spiritually valuable, even though your actions say you don't. For example, Jesus criticized the Pharisees because they claimed to point people toward God and to take his commands seriously while simultaneously currying personal gain. They were *not* pious; they only appeared to be so.

> **Falsely pious Christians eliminate sex when they speak of love, pretending that they are making "love" more holy.**

False piety tells us not to have public discourse about sex because it isn't proper or spiritual. Falsely pious Christians eliminate sex when they speak of love, pretending that they are making "love" more holy. But this view is mistaken, anti-biblical, sometimes an outright deception. The Bible devotes an entire book, Song of Songs, to the goodness of sexual union and intimacy.

This potent work makes the connection between conjugal love and sex, a connection lost within our churches and our culture. Observes Eugene Peterson, who translated this book from its original steamy Hebrew:

> The Song proclaims an integrated wholeness that is at the center of Christian teaching on committed, wedded love for a world that seems to specialize in loveless sex. The Song is a convincing witness that men and women were created physically, emotionally, and spiritually to live in love.

This sexually explicit material is resting on coffee tables throughout the world, within reach of children, and with no parental access code to keep them from opening it. According to God, it's a public document meant to be discussed and a behavior meant to be celebrated.

True to the motives of the falsely pious, those who say sex is solely a personal matter are hiding from something. At KDOV, when we'd air a program that encouraged increased sexual intimacy between husbands and wives, I would find myself in long and heated discussions with listeners who thought this was sinful. They were among the most rigid people I've ever met. Fearful people. People in hiding. *Hiding from intimacy.*

This is where the matter gets worse for Christian Nice Guys. Intimacy with God and sexual intimacy with our wives takes us out of Niceland, which is all about comfort and concealment. Sexual intimacy makes us vulnerable; vulnerability is risky; the church is *not* in love with risk. Instead of admitting their profound personal discomfort with intimacy, the falsely pious continue their anti-Christian assault upon the hearts of men, saying, then, that *God* thinks the public discussion of sex is unspiritual and immoral. What a distorted diversion—these same people usually argue for biblical inerrancy. Who do they think wrote the Song of Songs?

Intimacy with God and sexual intimacy with our wives takes us out of Niceland, which is all about comfort and concealment.

As long as they're still under the spell of fear and anxiety, CNGs can't stand risk either. However, here's where it gets interesting, and we make a huge mistake if we ignore this next point: *A Christian Nice Guy's desire for real sexual intimacy is often so strong that it can be a top motivator for him to confront his fears, to leave Niceland, and to become a Christian Good Guy instead.* The church should encourage, not hinder, this transformation.

> **Unfaithfulness and neglect are not separate categories—both are examples of disloyalty that simply differ by degree.**

False piety is a mindset that allows us to keep sinning while pointing our finger at others. For example, we repeat marriage vows that include proclamations of fidelity with words like *honor, protect,* and *care for;* we rightly condemn behavior that *breaks* these vows, but we fail to condemn behavior that *neglects* them.

The failure of wives to account for and handle their husband's normal and healthy sexual desires is a form of infidelity that *dis*honors their spouse. Unfaithfulness and neglect are not separate categories—both are examples of disloyalty that simply differ by degree. The damage from inaction can be just as dishonoring as the damage from action. Though silent and often invisible, the failure to act can be sinful, which Catholics emphasize in teaching their children about sins of omission, even as Protestants largely (sometimes exclusively) focus on sins of commission. Next time you're in church, count all the sinful actions you're encouraged not to carry out. Then listen for the sins associated with inaction (essentially the sins of passivity). The tally will likely shock you.

TWISTING GOD'S GOOD NEWS

People are forced to play myriad tricks to keep their false piety alive, and this sometimes includes twisting the Bible. I, and many other men, grew up believing that the Song of Songs is not as it appears—and this from a church that leans toward literal interpretation regarding most every other portion of Scripture. I was told in Sunday school—and from the pulpit as an adult—that the Song of Songs is *not* about the celebration of sexual intimacy and pleasure between a married Hebrew couple; it's really a metaphor that illustrates Christ's deep love for his church. Why we need such a "metaphor" when there's an entire Testament (the New) that attests to this loving relationship has never been well explained.

The allegorical (non-literal) interpretation has been tragic for Christian Nice Guys.

Think about it. A CNG hears about and reads the Song of Songs. He finds out that God embraces—*created*—his sexual desire and calls it good and right. Though he lives in a church culture that doesn't respect his heart's desire, he finally has a witness, a book, an author, a King of Kings, who understands his plight—he has received the biggest Amen of all!

Then he's told, "Not so fast. This book may seem straightforward to you, but it isn't as it appears—you're reading into it what you want to hear out of it." Talk about a sucker punch. The Bible begins to become a painful disappointment, and the church looks more and more like an enemy determined to ignore the male heart.

A BOLD CHALLENGE

I want a Christian band of married men to sing about the joys of wedded intimacy, the way God's Word delights in it through the Song of Songs and other books like Proverbs. I want it played over and over on Christian radio stations. I also want the lyrics to include some of the powerful biblical words used to describe sexual pleasure and intimacy. If Christians choose to believe that any of these words are unacceptable, then they must admit that God's Word is unacceptable.

Christian musicians: Blaze new trails, creating thunder by being honest about life, the way Jesus was honest and the way the Song of Songs treats our desires. Set to music the dynamic tension and release of sexual intimacy. Show us what it's like to be "restless in bed and sleepless through the night." Help us to experience what the beloved says in Song of Songs 3:1: "I longed for my lover. I wanted him desperately. His absence was painful" (THE MESSAGE).

When will Christian radio stations have the courage to play songs that signal to disillusioned men that the church both can change and is changing in their favor? As a former program director, I have the answer: When false piety freezes over.

We constantly complain about how the world treats sex recklessly and portrays marriage poorly. We have our own media through which to correct these corrosive caricatures, but we fail to fully or sometimes even adequately use them. Some programming is addressing this issue head on, but not our music, which has perhaps the greatest ability to stick in our minds and remain in our hearts.

Imagine if we sang about the joys of *responsible* sex, how it leads to higher thoughts, harmony in homes, healthy lives, secure children. Think about the redemptive good we would do if we sang of how married people actually have more sex, and more fulfilling sex, than singles do (despite pop culture's lies).

One friend, when he was agnostic, told me that he didn't like sex because of the "mess" it creates.

"Mess?!" I exclaimed. "That's dessert wine after a delicious meal! It's frosting on a cake!" The world too often reduces intimacy to raw sexual impulse; Christian culture often pretends this impulse doesn't exist.

Christian musicians: Write songs that help CNGs to see what they miss when they fail to enjoy their wives sexually; show them the damage this failure can perpetrate upon their souls and families. Shoot for the moon. (If you want, call me. We can write it together.) Do it without being crass and, equally important, without apology. Write boldly. Guide Christian Nice Guys down paths they're afraid to traverse for fear their fear will be made known. Again: "Encourage the timid, help the weak" (1 Thessalonians 5:14). CNGs can change if they're haunted with this unchanging reality; I'm living proof.

Men in general carry decades of shame for being men—it's part of the cultural legacy that defines us. We behave as if it's in our DNA. We've been told that we're the source of the world's problems because our very nature is wrong; this is why if a man upsets a woman for most any reason, he can be (and often is) labeled a pig by men and women alike. Desire for sexual intimacy is part of our nature, and the spurning of our masculine nature drives in the knife of shame even deeper.

It's worse for Nice Guys. Not only does their culture shame them for being *men,* but for some their messed-up childhoods make them feel ashamed for being *human.* Shame, double dose.

Christian Nice Guys have it the worst of all if they attend churches that uphold the popular myth that women are more moral, spiritual, and sensitive to God's calling. Think about it. If women are superior, and if they don't desire sexual intimacy as much, then the conclusion is clear: Moral people are less sexual. What prejudice! Christian men face an unholy trinity of shame—three powerful hands that slam down shame so heavily that many are emotionally slain by it. These forms of shame are not supported either by the Bible or by common sense. *None* of these forms should exist. They are a tri-fold lie.

Dr. Laura was right when she told me, "Men will do what women tolerate." What I'm asking, what I'm begging for on behalf of men in general and CNGs in particular, is for wives to do more than tolerate sex; learn to *share* in your husband's bliss. You and the church have the power to help the Christian Nice Guy out of his miry ghetto. You may not be able to change how he feels at work or how he feels toward his parents, but you can help him feel better at home. You can respect his legitimate desire, and the fact that this respect will honor him will breed respect in other areas of life as well. Jumpstart his masculinity and transformation, and when you do, you too will join the ranks of the Good Guy Rebellion.

> **If women are superior, and if they don't desire sexual intimacy as much, then the conclusion is clear: Moral people are less sexual.**

If the church continues to ignore essential male desires, it will do so to its own detriment and to the further destruction of home life, the exact opposite of what it's fighting hard to accomplish. If the church continues to ignore that men revolt from being told to have no real sexual desires and, worse, that they are somehow illegitimate, even perverted (as one former CNG's wife told him), they will look for it in other places, ways that actually are perverted.

The next beachhead to take is our culture's warped view of masculinity. That this conquest isn't easy is also what makes it fun.

CONFUSED TO VILIFIED: OUR CULTURE'S VIEW OF MASCULINITY

In the name of God, stop a moment, cease your work, look around you.

—LEO TOLSTOY

Women need men like fish need bicycles.

—YOUNG FEMINIST GLORIA STEINEM, WHO MARRIED A MAN IN 2002

There have always been Marvin Milquetoasts, men who are gentle and sensitive; their gentleness and sensitivity is right in many situations, but wrong when virtue demands that they be strong and straightforward instead.

Stemming from unprecedented societal shifts, the problem of all-sugar-no-spice males is worse than ever. *All* men receive a false, demeaning presentation of masculinity from our culture. This is due primarily to the absence of fathers (an estimated fifteen million American children currently live without a father in their home); other factors include the increase in divorce, homes headed by women, an educational system dominated by women, and radical feminism, which went from a battle for equality to guerilla warfare on the masculine soul. These and other unprecedented changes have meant boys are separated from their fathers and other significant male role models and have fallen prey to an anti-male prejudice. Countless boys have grown up—or are growing up—not knowing what it means to be a man and, worse, ashamed of the limited understanding they possess.

RADICAL FEMINISM

As even noted conservatives like James Dobson agree, feminism did once hold legitimate goals, but it distorted its original intent by attacking the very identity and purpose of men. We *need* to know and acknowledge this in order to chart a better course for men, women, and especially children, because the weak always suffer when the strong falter. Here are just a few examples of the life-draining misconceptions that have caused countless women to judge men—*masculinity*—as dangerous and destructive, and pass this virus from generation to generation.

> **Countless boys have grown up—or are growing up—not knowing what it means to be a man and, worse, ashamed of the limited understanding they possess.**

George, a frustrated CNG from New Mexico, worries for today's boys given how we degrade tough masculine behavior: "The media and the feminist movement have trivialized the role of men and fathers in a disgusting matter. Society has tamed and domesticated men and labeled anything other than 'nice' behavior as unacceptable. It breaks my heart to see schools force young boys to become feminized: sit in rows, do neat work, sit up straight. A boy who acts like a boy is labeled a troublemaker."

In her bestseller *The War Against Boys: How Misguided Feminism Is Harming Our Young Men*, Christina Hoff Sommers speaks of how many so-called experts throughout the last thirty or so years believed that "the problem with boys is that they *are* boys. . . . We need to change their nature. We have to make them more like . . . girls." Under the guise of helping girls, "Many schools adopted policies that penalize boys for simply being masculine."

While at the University of Oregon, I watched a group called Dykes from Hell (I'm not making this up), lesbians trained in martial arts, attempt to stop men from speaking at political gatherings by taking aggressive fighting stances in front of them. Men would be arrested if they did the same.

In class, I also watched a radical feminist stand up and shout down a professor of biopsychology who lectured on the scientific discoveries of gender-based biology, and how gender fosters different behaviors. She didn't debate him with opposing research; she stood up, raised her arms in the air, and bullied him off with an effective example of politically correct thought policing; radical feminists have perpetrated this ideological disaster for decades, helping to weaken and confuse sexual relations and identity.

Attending a meeting for Men Against Rape seemed like a no-brainer to me and my friend John, until the meeting began. It was led by the weakest of men, a guy whose answer to the revolting facts of rape fit perfectly into our culture's abominable view of men and its confusion of depraved male behavior with masculinity. He didn't advocate tougher laws and increased penalties; he didn't propose forming a group of committed men who would regulate and patrol rape hotspots around campus. He said that we men need to discard who we are; that we must strip ourselves of power, prowess, impulse, and desire. We men are the source of the world's pain, and therefore the remedy is simple: *Be men no longer.*

Entire generations of women have been told that not only are men disposable, they're also dangerous and worthy of ridicule. All the while, kids have been taking mental notes—boys, already more apprehensive about their world than girls, suffer the majority of nightmares and behavioral problems from stress and anxiety. They come to believe they don't deserve basic respect.

I've attended too many weddings of educated men and women, fresh from college, that worry me. The guy is docile and compliant, scrubbed of much that we'd call a masculine personality; the gal is guarded, suspicious-looking even while saying her wedding vows. They've had fine educations, they have enviable jobs, but they're already at war—and he never spends time with guys who aren't ashamed of being guys. "Those two are in for hell," I whisper to my wife.

Mocking men is good business in America. T-shirts, hats, and other merchandise bearing the slogan "Boys Are Stupid—Throw Rocks at Them" were once found in nearly 3,500 retail outlets worldwide; they show a little boy running away as stones fly at his head. Also available were "Boys Are Smelly—Throw Garbage Cans at Them" and "The Stupid Factory— Where Boys Are Made." Stores dropped the products only after a wave of protest led by radio personality Glenn Sacks during the *His Side* show. You probably never heard about this, because it didn't get much media coverage. But imagine the outcry if the merchandise had said to throw rocks and cans at girls.

Lionel Tiger, author of *The Decline of Males,* tells of how men have spiraled into "bewildered and lonely creatures," particularly by being increasingly marginalized from one of life's most precious decisions: fatherhood. "Contraceptive technology [increasingly] controlled by women" has made a growing number of men feel obsolete, "resulting in their unprecedented withdrawal from family systems."

When men *have* been allowed more say in the creation of children, they're told all that's needed is their sperm—forget about their protective love and their masculine guidance. This ludicrous trend has led (particularly throughout the last decade) to the derogatory concept of men as "Sperm Donors." Imagine the uproar if men referred to women merely as "Breeders."

> **Man's heart has been crushed by hearing and believing that he's not only unnecessary, but he's fully disposable.**

The destructive and insulting message that "in creating and upholding a family, you're not truly wanted or needed" has compelled men to live down to this vacuum of expectation and demand. Man's heart has been crushed by hearing and believing that he's not only unnecessary, but he's fully disposable.

SETTING THE RECORD STRAIGHT

Ready for the facts about how important fathers really are? The largest, most critical factor predicting whether a child will graduate from high school, attend college, avoid crime, reject drugs, or not become pregnant before eighteen is a father's presence in his or her life. According to a recent report by the Department of Health and Human Services (DHHS), "Fathers play a unique role in fostering the well-being of their children, not only through providership, protection, and guidance, but also through the way that they nurture the next generation."

However, there's a huge catch: *"A father's involvement with his children . . . is powerfully contingent on the mother's attitude"* toward him. Research on children consistently indicates that the father-child relationship, even more than the mother-child relationship, depends on the quality of the parents' relationship. See the snag? If for decades women have been told that they need a man "like fish need bicycles," then they have been encouraged to deny children an influence more integral and beneficial than good nutrition. This lowest-common-denominator view of masculinity has wrought unprecedented societal damage; radical feminism inarguably darkens a child's future.

The DHHS report makes it even clearer:

> Girls with active dads demonstrate higher levels of mathematical competence, and boys with more nurturing fathers display higher levels of verbal acumen. It is worth noting, of course, that girls tend to struggle more with math and boys tend to struggle more with language. Having an active, emotionally invested father appears to help children overcome the intellectual weaknesses typically associated with their sex. . . .
>
> Fathers are more likely to foster independent, exploratory behavior on the part of their children, compared to mothers. . . . Children

raised by engaged fathers are more comfortable exploring the world around them. . . .

A playful, challenging, and nurturing approach to fatherhood is associated with more self-control and pro-social behavior among children throughout the course of their lives. . . . One study of seventh graders found that boys who had close relationships with their fathers were more likely to control their feelings and impulses, to obey rules at school and home, and to make good moral judgments. . . . This same study found that boys with involved fathers had fewer school behavior problems and that girls had more self-esteem. . . .

Boys and girls who are exposed to the nurture of a father, and to see a father being nurturing to their mother and other adults, are much less likely to associate masculinity with predatory sexual behavior and hyper-aggressiveness. . . . Fathers help their children—especially their daughters—develop the self-control and the sense of self-worth that protects them from premature sexual intercourse and teenage pregnancy.

This is not isolated evidence; the documentation from research is out there. It's time to reclaim genuine masculinity *and* give man-hating feminism the boot.

MISUNDERSTANDING AND MISTREATING BOYS

As a longtime young boys' soccer coach as well as a father of two boys, I can state, with my right hand firmly on the Bible, that many well-intentioned women do not know what a boy really is. Some men don't understand either. Boys are often loud, silent, energetic, tired, kinetic, thoughtless, focused, absentminded, kind, or cruel. They can be open-throttled whirlwinds of paradox. They may have a driving need to romp on one another like coyotes in the evening—rolling, poking,

It's time to reclaim genuine masculinity *and* give man-hating feminism the boot.

tripping, laughing, and then tripping each other some more. They are, as psychologist John Rosemond said, "little aggressive machines." Says Dobson in *Bringing Up Boys,* "They often do really risky and dumb things for no apparent good reason."

Boys roll in mud puddles because they're there. They think it's funny to pants one another even as some mothers think they should go to prison for it. (I try not to smile.) They are sometimes cocky. They're wonderful in a smelly and demanding way. And if they don't have a man around who embraces being a man, they may become scared of their developing manhood, a powerful gift that growing boys should *not* feel condemned for experiencing.

Some mothers, whose affection for their boys I don't question, demand that their sons become little modern men: ever nice and always pleasant even to those who humiliate them at school, one mini-castration at a time. They would *never* tell their son to punch, as hard as he can, the schoolyard bully who's been belittling him for months, sometimes in front of girls.

I coached such a boy. Jack was quiet and wasn't great with words, so he rarely shared his thoughts. Then, during one drill, he told me about being bullied at school. I pulled him aside and asked him if he had a school buddy who would stand beside him. (It's no mystery why Jesus sent the disciples out in pairs: so they could lift each other up during tough times. Someone with a sidekick is less likely to get picked on than a loner. Studies show that two people can hold off a small crowd if necessary.)

He said he didn't.

So I asked him if he'd ever defended himself. "No, my mom says it's wrong." (I wanted to yell.)

Jack wasn't small, but he was slower than others and, given how hard it was for him to speak, I could see that he wasn't able to back down the bully with words alone—any words of protest would likely be used against him. Bullies are proficient at ridiculing those who live out of weakness and fear.

I saw how brave he could be on the soccer field. But he had no man in his home. I don't know why, and I'm not condemning his mother when I write this—I'm just laying out the facts. He was a pushover; he didn't have much masculine energy in him and it showed. Other kids picked on him because they could.

"It feels gross inside, doesn't it, when someone picks on you and gets away with it," I said, still remembering those days.

"Yeah," he said, looking down.

"You're strong, pal. And you're brave. I know you are."

Telling your son it's okay to let someone demean and diminish him, and that he is not to defend himself, is as bad as letting him ingest small amounts of poison, abuse of another kind. The poison doesn't kill him right away but increasingly erodes and internally damages him. In some cases this will begin to evidence itself through bizarre and self-destructive behavior. The shame he feels about himself will shut him down like a kill switch on a motor. Self-loathing is just a matter of time; his gradual "immunity" to the toxins will take the shapeless forms of numbness and fear.

I told Jack that he should defend himself next time. Stand up tall. Practice looking people in the eye. Learn in the mirror to make his face strong. Surprise the bully—if sensing that he's going to hit you as he's done in the past, get him first.

I told him that an effective place to hit is the stomach; it doesn't do any real damage at that young age, and it can quickly put someone down when necessary. I told him that every bully whose challenge I accepted backed down when I stood up physically. And that words alone don't get the job done, something adults forget when they're older.

Then I told his mother what I said.

Was I teaching Jack simply to work out his problems with his fists? I don't think so. Did I create a future bully? Unlikely—he wasn't the bullying type. Did I head off some future high school tragedy, another bitter-revenge Columbine attack? This is worth thinking long and hard about, but I don't know the answer.

Here's what I know. If you don't think you're valuable, others won't either. Former New York Mayor Rudy Giuliani calls this the "broken window" theory. He noticed that when broken windows go unrepaired in parts of the city, people assume no one really cares for the building; as a result, more people feel comfortable breaking more windows, and eventually criminals take over, all because no one valued it. This happens to people as well, writes Rabbi Shmuley Boteach: "Holiness has leaked out of our lives, and we, like abandoned buildings, are broadcasting our lack of self-esteem far and wide" (*Face Your Fears,* 183).

I taught Jack that he is not a punching bag for other people's problems or amusement. He is valuable, and he should protect his God-given value. Sometimes this includes not accepting abuse, the way Jesus didn't.

Jesus was illegally slapped by an official at his so-called trial, and instead of literally turning his other cheek to be slapped again, he stood up for himself and insisted that this abuser, this bully, follow legal protocol. *He* didn't follow protocol with the high priest; as recorded in John 18, when questioned about his teaching, Jesus said everything he taught was delivered publicly, that nothing was said in secret. "Why, then, do you question me?" he asked. To his attacker, Jesus responded, "If I have said anything wrong, tell everyone here what it was. But if I am right in what I have said, why do you hit me?"

> **Jesus' admonishment to "turn the other cheek" does not mean to accept abuse; it means to not return evil for evil.**

Jesus did not follow our church's current teaching about becoming a doormat and laying down personal rights; he assertively retained them and laid them down when *he* chose, not when anyone else required it. If standing up for yourself is sinful, then Jesus sinned—in that case, he either *should* have turned the other cheek or, if saying *anything,* should have done so by apology. This is another instance in which the theology of Nice gets us into trouble. Properly understood, *Jesus' admonishment to "turn the other cheek" does not mean to accept abuse; it means to not return evil for evil.* Protecting yourself verbally or physically is simply that, self-protection.

We often make more of a distinction between verbal and physical self-defense than is wise when it comes to boys, and one reason is that physical abuse is much more foreign to adults—even if they were once subject to it, most of them have lost touch with what it was like. It's naïve to tell a young boy that he can stop all abusers with words; kids live in a world where their boundaries are constantly being trampled upon by other kids, a trampling that, again, often doesn't happen to adults. Would a woman tell her husband to allow someone to beat him up in the workplace? Most likely not. But we tell our young men that such abuse is okay and somehow "Christian," a nonsensical discrepancy.

I've watched women suddenly become like pampered Hollywood war protestors and proclaim to boys that *all* fighting is wrong and never justified. They do not understand the world in which boys roam, and they inspire them to be timid. They want their boys to blindly respect *all* authority, even when their young noses smell corruption and when their perceptive eyes spot the deception of self-interest.

They forget, or maybe they don't know their Bibles well enough to see, that Jesus called Herod Antipas, a mighty authority figure, "that fox," which in today's language means *scumbag,* someone sly and underhanded. Irreverent language, especially spoken in frustration or anger, quickly earns the condemnation of women, who are then quick to close their eyes and point their finger. Hey, not everything in life is a term of endearment.

At the same time, almost miraculously, when women unleash shame-and-blame rhetoric upon their children or other children, this destruction is *more* than okay; it's justified, moral, necessary, and proper. A Christian man who utters irreverent words (I'm not talking about taking the Lord's name in vain) to describe the injustice he sees is condemned; a Christian woman who berates her children to the point of tears somehow thinks that to God the rough language is more offensive?

> When my children use irreverent language to describe injustice, I don't correct them. I wish more people did so describe the evil in this world.

When my children use irreverent language to describe injustice, I don't correct them. I wish more people did so describe the evil in this world. They would be more like Christ if they did; they would show that they are really alive, that they are reflecting the heart of the God who hates injustice. We are *truly* irreverent when we are indifferent toward the plight of others and the sins that curry God's wrath.

I've seen boys thoughtlessly hurt others, physically or verbally, usually through unrestrained aggression. They need to be corrected, but in such a way that they are not shamed.

Shame is what I see too many women do to boys, and it's got to stop: The Christian man is duty-bound not to let it happen to any of his children and, when he can, to stop it from happening to other children. Women shame boys in part because of their discomfort with the expression of raw male individuality. When you have opportunity, note how young girls often do the opposite when they get together: They homogenize, stripping themselves of unique identity in order to facilitate a highly valued connection.

Again, such female preference for trying to make the *other* (the masculine) become like *itself* (the feminine) is part of why female mishandling of a boy's heart is generally unintentional, lacking an understanding of authentic masculinity. However, such women often fortify their argument by using the Bible against boys, wrongly saying that *who they are* (rather than *their sinful actions*) is displeasing to God. I think some women resort to shame against boys when they despair over getting boys to do what they want; they pull out the big gun—shame—which, even if they know of its lethal effects, they may use simply to feel they are in control, and that they're getting boys to "behave." They behave all right, in ways we don't foresee; day by day, they gradually become fragmented Christian Nice Guys.

The effects of shame's shaky uncertainty are far-reaching. Atop the list is the complaint that men refuse to effectively lead their homes. Rock Bottomly, Senior Fellow at Focus on the Family Institute, says young men in particular have grown up in an age of cultural suspicion, making it difficult to exercise any leadership without winning someone's ire. "Men are scared and confused," he says.

ANDROGYNOUS NO MORE

There was a time when we made too much of the differences between men and women. And women usually suffered. Now our culture has worked double time to get us to believe there are no differences between the sexes. For example, some point to the fact that the DNA of men and women differs only by 1 to 2 percent. This doesn't sound like much, until you realize that this is the same percentage of difference between women and female chimpanzees.

We're different physically, emotionally, and psychologically. Mothers possess a greater ability to understand infants and children; they are more responsive to the "distinctive cries of infants; they are better able than fathers, for instance, to distinguish between a cry of hunger and a cry of pain" (Brad Wilcox, speech in Qatar). Mothers release pepetide oxytocin, a hormone that exists only during pregnancy and breast-feeding, that makes them more interested in bonding with children and engaging in nurturing behavior.

Fathers, by contrast, excel when it comes to discipline, play, and exhorting their children to embrace life's challenges. Physical play is far more important than most realize, promoting "social skills, intellectual development, and a sense of self-control" (Wilcox, speech). Fathers' playful side teaches their children how to regulate their feelings and behavior as they interact with others. Children who roughhouse with fathers usually learn quickly that biting, kicking, and other such actions are not acceptable.

Fathers are more likely than mothers to encourage their children to take up difficult tasks, to seek out fresh experiences, and to endure pain and hardship without yielding. "The bottom line is that fathers excel in teaching their children the virtues of fortitude, temperance, and prudence for life outside their family" (Wilcox, speech).

The contemporary androgynous impulse doesn't recognize the unique talents of the genders, dogmatically refusing to recognize the facts as laid out by sociologist David Popenoe's conclusion:

While mothers provide an important flexibility and sympathy in their discipline, fathers provide ultimate predictability and consistency. Both dimensions are critical for an efficient, balanced, and humane child-rearing regime. (*Life Without Father*)

Or as the publication *Child Development* found: Children of parents who engaged in sex-typical behavior, where the mother was more responsive/nurturing and the father was more challenging/firm, were more competent than children whose parents did not.

If the value of fatherhood continues to be negated, the observation of former U.S. Senator Daniel Patrick Moynihan will continue to haunt us:

A community that allows a large number of young men (and women) to grow up in broken families, dominated by women, never acquiring any stable relationship with male authority . . . that community asks for, and gets, chaos.

Men and women communicate differently, look at information differently, and have different basic desires. After a man becomes a Christian, much of this doesn't change, and it shouldn't—he's still a man, complete with innate masculine desires and preferences. I often wonder if the conflicts between men and women that we regularly discuss in church have more to do with gender differences than with spiritual differences.

> **I often wonder if the conflicts between men and women that we regularly discuss in church have more to do with gender differences than with spiritual differences.**

Every guy ends up asking himself the question *Why did I marry?* at some point (often after a fight). For one thing, honestly, I was sick of hanging around guys; I wanted that delicious, mystifying, catlike female strangeness to be grafted into my life. I craved her mysterious ways and, let's just say, her other attractive attributes.

My wife, after fifteen years of marriage, still intrigues me. I don't quite get her sometimes and, while I usually like this fact, one reality is that we simply have different priorities on issues of importance. As suggested above, this isn't even always due so much to our being two very different *individuals* as it is to our being different *genders*.

A mother once came to my door and told me her son had left his shirt at our house—she wanted me to retrieve it. I had work on my mind, and at any rate I had no idea what she was talking about, so my immediate response was a sort of glazed stare. I don't monitor clothing around here; unless it has functioning strobe lights attached, it's just one rag lost in a mountain of cloth. The best I can do is being fairly sure that all three of my kids have clothing on when they go to school (and I couldn't even tell you what color).

My wife wasn't home, but if she had been, she'd have known where that shirt was the way an owl knows how to locate a mouse. She'd also recall the shade, size, brand, style, and slogan (if any) on the front. It would likely be folded perfectly and put in a darling little sack with pretty plastic stuff around it, and perhaps on top would rest a card, thanking this woman for another gift from five years ago. I think this is great, I really do. It just isn't me.

Because Sandy was *not* home, I told the lady I had no clue where the shirt was and wouldn't have any idea where to begin. When I invited her in to search, she looked at me indignantly, and I realized, *She thinks I should know and that I'm negligent because I don't.*

I monitor what my kids are thinking, whether they need protection, in what ways they're struggling, how I can help them with their difficulties. It is not my nature to keep track of clothes, and I'm not about to add that one to my radar. I wasn't having a hard time processing that; I was irritated because she was trying, silently, to shame me.

I was tempted to respond in kind, to ask, "Do you know what weight of oil is in your car right now? Want me to tell you?" But that wouldn't have done either of us any good, and besides, she was one of those women who believe in their hearts—like Debra on *Everybody Loves Raymond*—that if men would just adopt female sensibilities, this world would be so much better. (I know her husband. God help him.)

Recently at church my pastor announced an upcoming demolition party: We're putting a new ceiling on the sanctuary and the old one has to go. I was all ears—in fact, smiling from ear to ear. I'm sure the non-intellectual look on my face said, *Mmm, Paul likes to destroy.* My hands nearly sweat with excitement. In my mind I'd already donned my hardhat, pulled on my Carhart jeans, and grabbed my trusty sledgehammer. It was like an unexpected Christmas present.

I turned to the woman sitting next to me and said, "I can't wait. I love breaking things." She gave me a bemused look, replied, "I'm glad someone does." That she showed zero interest was fine with me—more demolition for me to enjoy!

> **Marriages, congregations, and societies are at their best when femininity *and* masculinity are respected and appreciated.**

I did *not* glare at her and say, "For shame—how can you call yourself a Christian woman and not partake in the Lord's important work?" I didn't call her a freeloader or accuse her of being morally deficient, or quote Paul's words about the necessity of all people pulling their weight. I didn't hold her to an alien standard and condemn her for being true to her inclinations.

Marriages, congregations, and societies are at their best when femininity *and* masculinity are respected and appreciated. This is why I'm concerned by the move within some Christian circles to abolish all forms of dating. While it's an imperfect arrangement, in what better way are we to obtain greater understanding and appreciation for the gender so unique and so different from our own? (Books alone won't cut it.) Could it be that we've so bought the unisex lie that now we think there's no learning curve?

MASCULINITY AND SENSITIVITY: NO DICHOTOMY

One common misconception about masculinity is that somehow it's devoid of sensitivity and tenderness; here we are hurt by our lack of acumen and appreciation for paradox. Think, for instance, about the Cross: How could such incomprehensible love and rejection ever be conjoined? How might the ultimate humiliation result in the ultimate glory? How can agonizing death lead to everlasting life? Two extreme traits that *seem* to contradict and conflict don't always cancel each other out; the mystery of paradox enhances life with richness, beauty, breadth, and freedom.

Said Søren Kierkegaard, "Paradox is really the *pathos* of intellectual life, and just as only great souls are exposed to passions, it is only the great thinker who is exposed to what I call paradox." To know God well, we *must* develop a viable understanding of paradox, for without it we undercut our lives with destructive ideas. In this case, masculinity is reduced to machismo—a perversion exemplified by so-called pro wrestling. This is the belief that masculinity is limited to physical struggle, a notion that if actually true, would mean we are in both the simplest and cruelest of worlds.

The man of the feminist/New Age ideal is also devoid of paradox—he's mushy and responsive without discernibly initiating through action and strength; he has discarded physical struggle and physical protection as animalistic and crass. (As the theory goes, that's something *other* men do—lesser, uneducated men, who've not yet been enlightened.) We can all thank God that Winston Churchill and all the brave men who defied and defeated the ominous twentieth-century threat of fascism weren't so squishy-nosed.

Writes Leon Podles:

> Jesus was willing to accept pain without any attempt to desensitize himself. He chose the twelve, knowing that one was to betray him, and felt the pain of the betrayal—*Do you betray the Son of Man with a kiss?* He loved the people to whom he had been sent, weeping over the Jerusalem that rejected him. . . .
>
> On the cross, he refused the drug that was traditionally offered to criminals to dull their pain. He wanted to taste the pain of human life and death to the full; he chose freely to taste it, in an exercise of the highest courage. . . . His tenderness and compassion were not a grafting of feminine characteristics onto a masculine personality, but

rather a profound expression of masculinity. (Podles, *The Church Impotent,* 80)

Masculinity means, for one thing, that we men push past our fears of emotional depth and we weep, as Jesus did, when it's appropriate.

My eyes remained dry while watching movies for most of my life. Like many guys, I kept my feelings to myself not because I was tough, but because I was weak. The fear that owned me turned me into a passive man, someone who went through life with a smile on his face while avoiding life's highs and clipping its lows—crying in public qualified as a major low. *My goal wasn't living and loving; it was comfort and control.*

I'm not that man anymore. When I watched *The Passion of the Christ* with my son Elliot, I needed no effort or attempt; how could I not weep when watching my innocent, perfect Savior being treated with such barbarism and evil and yet responding with such selfless love?

Though my eyes welled up through much of the film, I lost it when Jesus fell, again, carrying his immense cross. When Mary, his mother, broke through the crowd to comfort him. When Jesus recognized her through his bludgeoned eyes and told her to watch as he made all things new.

His loving sacrifice in the face of such torture and injustice set off a series of eruptions inside me like the implosive demolition of old buildings. I dropped my head and wept. As a Christian Nice Guy I dared not give in to the temptation to weep; as a CNG, I kept my feelings in by keeping life out.

————

Elliot's left hand was in my right. He tightened his grip and stroked my forearm with his other hand.

"It's about love, Elliot. We're supposed to love," I whispered.

"Right," he said.

Though I come from men whose tears should have overflowed but didn't, I released pure, clean tears of sadness—honest, redemptive, oddly relaxing tears that came from *knowing* that God really is on my side.

The only tears I ever saw my father shed were far different.

I was around Elliot's age when I was making too much noise with a basketball, throwing it on the roof and letting it bounce down to me, then trying to catch it before it hit the ground. It was sunny and perfect outside. But inside, unknown to me, Mom lay under another migraine. She was trying to rest, and her rest didn't come easily.

When my father came home after another sweaty day of painting homes, he must have gotten an earful. He came back outside with a huge pair of solid metal scissors, and I ran wildly as he plunged them deep into that basketball's skin, an unforgettable display of frustration and anguish from a life that wasn't working out and felt like too much to bear. Foundational cracks had rifted and revealed themselves, like the fault line beneath our Southern California home, hit by earthquakes both physical and emotional.

As I watched from the side of the house, my cheek scratched from the stucco, my father severed that basketball clean in half. Then he sat down, buried his face into his tired, freckled hands, and made the noises of a deaf person asked to speak but unable to form words. He grunted and groaned. He trembled. He exuded pain. He coughed shards of sound that seemed to be cutting his throat. His eyes flashed wet and red with anguish. And the episode ended almost as quickly as it began.

I just put those scissors down. Somehow I inherited it, this Italian-made, twelve-inch long piece of metal with the word I. PHYDE on the face. It comes to a stylish yet menacing point, the kind they hand the antagonist in movies. A frustrated man could stab a boy with it, or a dog that barks forever after a wearisome day at work. It's an instrument that a good man might use to leak out his frustrations in a Willy Loman–like flash flood of desperation, a shiny medium through which to pour his will and feel some oily power flow, healing, so it might seem, the befuddled tenure of his life.

I hold this heavy metal in the same kind of hands today: white, freckled, worn, though not as worn as his. Though I didn't marry the same kind of woman, I know marriage woes. He traversed a river full. I, a brook that grows dryer by the year, and I consider myself fortunate. I can empathize now with his darkness. He had no one, no friend, brother, priest, neighbor, not even a bartender to whom he could really turn. He was trapped in his guy box like so many men, then as now. I'm not.

Within a short car drive or quick cell phone call, I can share my soul with a tribe of men who won't tell on me regardless of what leaks out of my troubled head. That's one of the blessings of fellowship.

When I hold the scissors, I can smell my father again: the paint and the thinner, the sandpaper and the wood dust. His immigrant sweat unencumbered by deodorant. It's slightly sweet and mostly savory. I would bottle it if I could and call it Working Man. I think Steve McQueen would be the best pitch person, but I think my dad would want Sinatra instead, who defined what it meant to be a man for at least two generations. Blue Eyes is fine with me.

I smell him, and an ancient longing begins again. This haunting has an air of holiness to it. I want him back. Tears follow. Something is unfinished in my head. I want to tell him I'm sorry and that I wish a little boy playing with a ball in his backyard didn't add to his domestic woes. But such things do. Everyday home life swirls around itself to create a congealed mass that eventually becomes extraordinary. My play, that ball, those scissors, her migraine—they are glued to one another like letters in a word. This was a painful word.

> **I had a personal philosophy that also hinders many other men from experiencing the passion, and embracing all, of their masculinity: *Emotions suck. Avoid them.***

The day of the Mighty Scissors burned into the film of my mind and helped form a personal philosophy that also hinders many other men from experiencing the passion, and embracing all, of their masculinity: *Emotions suck. Avoid them.*

Truthfully, I tell you all this to give you hope and courage. It's possible to break these ties that bind generations of men from Christ's abundant life. There is such a thing as a cleansing, healthy cry, the kind that doesn't alarm, but rather invites another into a deeper layer of life. My son wasn't frightened by my display; he was fortified by it. I pray that he demonstrates the same to my future grandchildren.

Ridding our lives of emotion is cruel to those around us. For example, because men often represent the weight of life to their kids, this weight *must* include feelings, lest our children become caricatures of the fabricated Jesus. Without emotions, they will go into life half-powered, and they will suffer from lack of motivation and inability to connect with others, leaving them weak and isolated.

I want my tears to liberate my sons so that they embrace the entire masculine spectrum, from tender to tough. I seek to be honest with my concerns, letting them see some (though not all) of my struggles, so that they'll better handle their own; making sure they hear me ask God for forgiveness, and making sure I ask them as well.

I like my tears of sorrow and joy. Seeing adorable babies at church, bobbing their big heads around, pretty much guarantees I won't be hearing much of the sermon. I can't take my eyes off their beauty; I want to hold them and whisper kind words to them. Dr. Laura writes that "without an awareness and acceptance of feelings, a male doesn't become a man, he becomes a male cartoon—the animation required for humanness *is feelings*" (*10 Stupid Things Men Do*, 282).

FRED ROGERS: NOT A NICE GUY

Gentleness *is* a virtue. I remember how warm I felt as a troubled kid, watching Mr. Rogers. He blessed me with his gentle ways, and he helped to settle my anxious, battered heart.

You didn't expect me to defend Mr. Rogers, did you? Well, Fred Rogers was a *Good* Guy—a Nice Guy would never have worked so hard to love others. "Discipline was his very strong suit," said his wife, Joanne, after his death. "If I were asked for three words to describe him, I think those words would be courage, love, and discipline—perhaps in that very order" (Fred

Rogers, *The World According to Mr. Rogers: Important Things to Remember,* 7).

Nice Guys are weak in all three of these vital areas; they would buckle under the unfair jabs thrown his way. Fred Rogers was lampooned for his loving ways; he knew it, and he continued anyway. Though he took great risks, they didn't show. He didn't *want* them to show, because he wanted to impart the gift of stability to children who lacked this critical nourishment.

He fought, through gentle means, against bigotry and injustice toward kids. Joanne says he struggled to come up with the exact words to reach their hearts. Again, a Nice Guy wouldn't have (*nor* would he seek) the inner strength to undergo such labor: "He was able to find the courage and determination to use his knowledge and talents—and, in fact, his whole life—in the service of children."

People who put down Fred Rogers reveal their own lack of perspective and understanding, for he was no fake Nice Guy—his love was real and pure. "Love isn't a state of perfect being," he reminded us. "It is an active noun, like 'struggle'" (Rogers, 53).

> **Love isn't a state of perfect being. It's an active noun, like *struggle*.**

Actually, he didn't have to tell us—he showed us. Then again, however, perhaps he did need to tell most of us in writing, for we still don't respect his redemptive work in a way that honors what he did with his life. On the holiday we should name after him, we should all raise a glass and recite what he knew was true:

> It's not the honors and the prizes and the fancy outsides of life that ultimately nourish our souls. It's the knowing that we can be trusted, that we never have to fear the truth, that the bedrock of our very being is firm. (Rogers, 26)

Simultaneously, we must acknowledge that gentleness and kindness are not the only virtues we're called to embrace, as C. S. Lewis explained:

> For about a hundred years we have so concentrated on one of the virtues—"kindness." . . . Such lopsided ethical developments are

not uncommon, and other ages too have had their pet virtues and curious insensibilities. (*A Year With C. S. Lewis,* 282)

We must also embrace our inner policeman, who uses the level of force necessary to ensure the peace. To Christians in general this sounds sacrilegious—we're so often reminded to pick up our crosses and follow Jesus. But how have we ignored that he picked up a whip as well? To the pacifist who will point out that he never used it, I then ask, what was the purpose of that display? False bravado? Self-conceit? *No.* Protection is more than the use of force—it's also the threat of carrying (and willingness to carry) it out.

And we are indeed seeing more and more acceptance of masculinity's essence, even to the point where it's no longer taboo to make extremist feminism the butt end of a joke. That's why Professor Camille Paglia can get away with saying, "Whiffle [whine and wheeze and snuff and sniffle]: The annoying scratchy sound made by weepy feminists as they lament the sufferings of women and, hound-like, sniff out evidence of male oppression."

Radical feminism was and has been afforded social grace, and that age of grace is ending. Even the old guard is changing its mind. Gloria Steinem, among the biggest names in that powerful but fleeting movement, once said that women don't need men, yet she married one during a time in which she could have married a woman instead. She may say that this doesn't signify "need" but "want"; though there is a difference, the difference is tiny. The tide is turning, and not a decade too soon.

> **Protection is more than the use of force—it's also the threat of carrying (and willingness to carry) it out.**

NICE GUY, NAÏVE GUY: HOW BEING NICE HURTS MEN AT WORK

Fear is the faith that it won't work out.
— UNKNOWN

Defensive strategy never has produced ultimate victory.
— DOUGLAS MACARTHUR

Christian men who adhere to the gentler, trendier, and more extreme messages within the church regarding how they should behave have a lot of misconceptions to overcome. Few are more pivotal than in the workplace, where such messages consistently keep them down.

As explained earlier, Christian men with abuse and related issues in their background formed a naïve philosophy of life when they were young boys: "If I live small, then my troubles will be few." It's a prisoner-like approach that seems to make sense when all odds are against you.

Unknowingly, though, CNGs bring this defensive, incomplete, and naïve attitude into adult life even when their coast is clear. They're like hunkered-down South Pacific island villagers who were never told World War II had ended, so they stayed underground, ever vigilant of invaders who would never come. In our society, such diminishing, defensive behavior and posture can be more difficult to ascertain and address. Only by discarding specific misunderstandings and false beliefs will the Christian Nice Guy gain strength in this area of his life and come out of his bunker to chart a vastly better career.

THE TRAP OF "PERFECT" WORK

CNGs believe they must do everything *perfectly,* which they think is insurance against criticism. By contrast, this is often a form of self-sabotage and a covert way of avoiding legitimate or constructive criticism, because no one is actually capable of this ideal. As common sense reveals, perfection is an earthly illusion and is used as an excuse not to complete workplace *or* kingdom-purpose projects.

In his desperate quest for avoidance, the Nice Guy hides his mistakes, even ones with little if any consequences. This further weakens him by hindering him from learning life's cumulatively valuable lessons that can lead to greater maturity, ability, and, eventually, income for him and his family. *Refusal to acknowledge mistakes severely inhibits excellence;* conversely, Wolfgang Puck confesses, "I learned more from the one restaurant that didn't work than from all the ones that were successes."

Nice Guys are stuck. The workplace passes them by. They see it. They blame those around them. Including (or especially) God.

These men have a hard time asking for help, because they think it shows weakness. That they feel they must always appear in control also limits them—they often try to shoulder too much responsibility and have great difficulty delegating. Burnout is their common recompense.

> **Nice Guys are stuck. The workplace passes them by. They see it. They blame those around them. Including (or especially) God.**

Such behavior also has a strong influence on the Nice Guy's relationships at work, because people aren't drawn to perfection—whether deep down or up top, they know it's a veneer. Workplace friendships and alliances are born from shared interests and problems;

projecting an image of perfection only makes you appear slippery, uninteresting, and untrustworthy.

CNGs: Don't let a job well done fall prey to the illusion of perfect work. You have a right to be wrong, and nothing teaches and matures you like mistakes.

THE DANGERS OF FORMULA-LIVING

Because they feel they don't have the skills necessary to succeed at work, Christian Nice Guys are prone to look to formulas and other people's opinions as road maps through the workplace's troubled terrain. I'm not talking about gaining insight and wisdom into ways of earning a living, which is smart. I'm talking about a belief that there's an ironclad and perfect plan that, once found, will answer all the major problems of work life. No such guide exists.

The temptation to fall for such an appealing but deceptive message is alive and well within Christian publishing. Though the Bible provides clear directives by way of moral and ethical behavior, it doesn't always provide a paint-by-number solution when life hurls a vocational curve ball. Sometimes following another's path through hard times may not be anywhere near the best for you.

It's so tempting to run into the arms of formula-thinking when staring over the cliff of the unknown; what God wants us to do is run into his arms in order to build our faith. Confusion is not always a problem to be solved—it can be a detour that eventually leads to a better life.

> **Confusion is not always a problem to be solved—it can be a detour that eventually leads to a better life.**

One of the events that cured me from thinking there's always a clearly delineated path through jagged workplace topography was listening to Oval Office recordings. I heard presidents groping in the darkness of history in the making, as when President Kennedy wrestled with the Cuban Missile Crisis. JFK and his advisors languished over taking chances with no assurance of victory, the way I do. Another man's anguish had never felt so good, because I realized that my suffering isn't unique. There *aren't* two kinds of men, those who know how to handle everything thrown their way and those like me who don't: We all suffer the same maddening fate. Call me crazy, but this gives me hope.

Another was reading the journal John Steinbeck kept while writing *The Grapes of Wrath*, considered by many to be the best American novel. Steinbeck was brilliant, but you wouldn't think so from reading *Working Days*, in which he often laments that he's writing nothing good and that he's just "pretending" to be a writer. One of America's premier literary figures (and he's nowhere near the only one) fought against self-doubt and worry. He suffered and he struggled, the way I do, the way everyone does when trying to do something purposeful.

One day Steinbeck writes, "I can do it. I feel very strong to do it" (25); then, "I must not be weak"; then, "Tomorrow I will have to fight my willpower." He pushes for months, till he writes on October 19, 1935, "I am sure of one thing—it isn't the great book I had hoped it would be. It's just a run-of-the-mill book. And the awful thing is that it is absolutely the best I can do." Then he won the 1940 Pulitzer Prize, the cornerstone of his 1962 Nobel Prize.

Smart career behavior accepts life's innate mysteries; these can infuse you with needed flexibility and creativity, qualities that formula-living often hinders. As seen in the movie *Apollo 13*, sometimes you have to ad lib, or you aren't going to make it.

BE CAREFUL WITH "CHRISTIAN" FAMILY BUSINESSES

CNGs need to be cautious about the kind of workplace they enter; as explained earlier, they are drawn toward abusive settings because such treatment feels normal. Though there is no Job Charming out there, some workplaces and positions are better than others. One to check out with painstaking scrutiny is a business run by a Christian and his or her family.

Now, I know I may have instantly earned your ire, but please hear me out. I'm not going to write that *all* Christian businesses are troublesome—some are good and healthy. I *will* cover why CNGs need to proceed with caution: There's a powerful lore within Christian circles that describes family-run business as the true biblical model and argues that, pragmatically, it's the ideal setup. It may be—for family. If you're not family, there are a few things you need to know.

I take no pleasure in saying the following, but I must, because it will help numerous CNGs: Some of the worst horror stories I've heard and seen involve companies run by evangelical Christians. I know that sounds harsh, and I wish I could avoid this conclusion, but it's true. Some are run by wishy-washy, manipulative, dishonest men who tell one person one thing and another something different. They also refuse to confront obvious examples of workplace inequality and abuse, often on behalf of their own family.

Working only for Christians can be a particular weakness for CNGs. They may think that a "Christian" workplace is somehow immune to the regular stresses and strains of business—mighty attractive to people who will do almost anything to avoid conflict.

> **Being a Christian doesn't automatically qualify anyone to lead. Good bosses are good bosses—you'll see it in their actions.**

Those workplaces *aren't* immune to such realities. Work is hard. That's why it's called labor. And some Christians who aren't well suited to lead a business will play all sorts of games to hide this fact. Don't judge them if you're employed by them; leadership is difficult work, something Nice Guys are adept at avoiding. At the same time, though, realize that being a Christian doesn't automatically qualify anyone to lead. Good bosses are good bosses—you'll see it in their actions. Martin Luther declared, "I'd rather be ruled by a wise Turk [a pagan] than a foolish Christian."

CONFRONTING WORKPLACE PROBLEMS

If you work for a family-run business and discover favoritism and other injustices, think long and hard about what you will do next, because you will likely end up on the losing end of whatever goes down. Blood is thicker than high-sounding principles, whether they have a Christian veneer (as opposed to actual principles) or not. Family members know the boss's weaknesses better than any other employee; some may play upon them masterfully, which can become a beguiling kind of mind control. You, the non-family guy, may be left with little if any recourse when you see (and especially express) how blatant the favoritism really is.

There's another word for this kind of unfairness: *nepotism*. The words synonymous with it are far from virtuous, including *corruption, bribery, graft, venality,* and other ugly terms that describe ugly situations for CNGs.

Nice Guys often rage (inside) when they experience this kind of injustice, partly because it reminds them of what they experienced as kids. Making matters worse is their undetected desire to be taken care of by others. Even though it can be painful, Christian Nice Guys must know this: No one is responsible for you or your paycheck other than you and the aid you allow God to give you. Your boss doesn't owe you anything other than compensation for what you provide. He's not your daddy—no one is but God above. This is hard to hear when you are still under the spell of fear and anxiety, but believe me when I say it has the power to bring liberation and peace.

AskJeeves.com is even more pessimistic about family-run workplaces, saying that a non-family whistle-blower has slight odds of success if he confronts such favoritism:

> Sure the company may do the right thing (sometimes reluctantly) and get rid of the family member. . . . However, the working level managers/supervisors are likely to then "make life miserable" for the whistle-blower and retaliate, sometimes in bold and sometimes in subtle ways. . . .
> Bottom line . . . unless the nepotism situation is directly depriving you of money for food, shelter, clothing, transportation, etc., then it is better to "see no evil, hear no evil, speak no evil"!

Such workplace confrontations can backfire very quickly. Alliances you thought were firm may break apart at crucial moments. People may run and hide, leaving you high and dry and possibly unemployed. This is a staple of the Christian Nice Guy work experience, especially in ministry (and that's a whole other book).

Timing is critical when fighting hypocrisy and other forms of injustice; God's Word reveals this when it says, "Do not withhold good from those who deserve it, *when it is in your power to act*" (Proverbs 3:27, emphasis added). This takes wisdom, skill, and a righteous form of cunning, qualities Jesus possessed, as seen, for example, when he didn't take the bait put before him by the Pharisees and Herodians. They wanted to snag him with his own words by having him answer a loaded question: Should they pay taxes to Caesar or not? (Matthew 22:17–22).

"Why are you trying to trap me?" he replied. His answer—"Give to Caesar what is Caesar's and to God what is God's"—stunned his audience. It would stun us in church today, not because it's cunning and shrewd but because it's not "nice." This kind of confrontation is the work of a *good* (not a nice) person.

Family bonds go deeper than most CNGs realize. If you do choose to work in a place that contains some or many of these precarious elements, don't lose your common sense, and do keep your résumé up to date, because you will likely need it. Save money every month. Share your concern with your wife, while also trying not to whine too much; you need to be on the same page if and when both shoes drop. Keep your debt load down so you can afford to be without a job for a time.

Family-run businesses are not for those who think everyone plays by the same rules. Phil from Florida, who has dealt well with his CNG-thinking in the workplace, now sees how naïveté hurt him. "I thought [because I lived] according to the Ten Commandments and other truths in the Bible, others lived by them as well. That was a mistake."

My advice to Phil is, do good work. Don't be dishonest in return. At the same time, don't be naïve either. People sin; by and large they are particularly good at it when family and money are involved.

WORKPLACE IS FAMILY?

One of the most brutal Christian Nice Guy mistakes is to think of the workplace in terms of family. Many CNGs come from troubled homes, and they long to be surrounded by people who really care for them, looking to colleagues and superiors to fulfill basic needs they've never had filled. This is understandable in principle, but disastrous in practice.

When CNGs think about the workplace as family, they are likely to give far more than that for which they are compensated; when they later begin to admit and examine this, they find their emotions have been further damaged. They are also prone to over-sacrifice themselves at work; they sense it in their gut, but they tell themselves they're being Christlike when they go without and come up short.

Do good work. Don't be dishonest, but don't be naïve either. People sin; by and large they are particularly good at it when family and money are involved.

This is foolish. *Here's* being Christlike: getting paid for the work you've done, and then, voluntarily—by volition, from your own will—taking your hard-earned money and giving it away, if that's what *you* choose. There's nothing Christlike or kind or good about being taken advantage of without choice. Those who fail to implement self-respect, and require respect from others, are prone to reap a harvest of dust, leaving their families open to economic devastation.

BEWARE OF DISSIMULATION

Humorist Studs Terkel referred to the workplace as "violence," which ain't exactly humorous. And I wouldn't take it that far. But I do think he's on to something that CNGs need to understand; they already enter the workplace with a defensive posture, a posture that will change once they renew their minds and unshackle their hearts. (More on that later.)

I wish I would have spotted dissimulation (pretense, deceit) earlier in my working life—there would have been so much less turmoil in my head and home if I had. *Dissimulation means to disguise one's true intentions;* it's a dressed-up way to say that someone is lying. "To know how to dissimulate," said Cardinal Richelieu way back in 1641, "is the knowledge of kings." Christian Nice Guys: Know that not much has changed in the centuries since.

Church culture tells men to give an earnest answer to every question posed—regardless of its intent and regardless of how Jesus handled such trickery.

I once had a job with regular staff retreats, which were designed (I was told, anyway) to bring about workplace unity. In order to create this unity, people were encouraged to speak their minds and answer questions honestly. It exasperated me that I was willing to speak truthfully about the frustrations and grumbling that I heard all around me, while others wouldn't say a single word in an official context. Then I found out why. My comments would be used against me months later, which probably had happened to my co-workers in years past before they wised up.

The questions weren't designed to bring about team unity, they were designed to obtain self-professed flaws and weaknesses, which could later be utilized to someone else's benefit (against me). I was being suckered by dissimulation and its close buddy, pretense.

Even so, I held tightly to my church-ordained script. Year after year I kept revealing myself, thinking somehow my church-encouraged earnestness would reform the problem. It didn't. I set myself up for needless suffering by choosing to be a pawn in someone else's selfish game. Innocent as a Dove: 1, Wise as a Serpent: 0.

Jesus shows us a better way.

When I learned to tell portions of the church, and so-called "men's ministries," to talk to my hand, life improved. As shown earlier, I noticed that Jesus didn't behave like a "typical Christian man" when confronted with entrapping questions—he either didn't answer them or he threw out penetrating inquiries of his own.

Jesus was wise as a serpent when he walked among us. He laid down his God-given dignity, his precious life, and his iron will *when he chose.* He went along with the cross-bound conspiracy against him, not because he didn't see the sham miles away, but because it was part of his redemptive mission. After drawing unwanted attention to Judas, the primary conspirator, with sustenance at the Last Supper, he told him, "What you are about to do, do quickly"—even telling his betrayer what to do! The irony of his kiss was not lost on Jesus—he bamboozled the bamboozlers and even then got the last laugh. Why hasn't *this* been the subject of a three-point sermon? Because even though it's how Jesus behaved, we say it's not "Christian." (How can something not be Christian and yet be as Christ would say or do?)

When we aren't wise as serpents, our home life suffers. Our kids are anxious and neglected. Our wife feels unprotected and resorts to control and criticism. The dog is kicked. All of this because wisdom is not imparted from leaders who are afraid of what will happen if they portray a complete Jesus.

The workplace has more than its fair share of dissimulation, and, contrary to your idealistic leanings, you aren't likely to change this, so be very careful if you confront it. This is why I keep harping on how Jesus said to be shrewd as serpents. If Christian ministers took this admonition seriously, they would be creating life-giving sermons like "How to Tell When Someone's Lying to You," messages that CNGs desperately need to hear. They often don't know when people are lying to them—they really don't. Their default setting is to take people at face value, which includes flattery, and though this may sound sweet, it isn't wise—it's naïve. Christ told Peter not to be naïve, and it's fair to say he wants us to be wise as well.

Please understand, I'm *not* saying we should go around committing the inverse mistake and thereby think everyone is guilty of all kinds of mischief; that's not usually the case. We've all met dismal people who see life through this filter; dark-cloud co-workers who are guarded and leery of friend and foe alike, seeing cliques and conspiracies everywhere. I *am* pointing out that there is no virtue in being a pawn either. A purpose-driven life demands action that's in line with your calling and your mission, not part of someone else's agenda—working in a way that provides well for them and their family, but not for you and yours.

MEMORIZE THIS PHRASE

> **A purpose-driven life demands action that's in line with your calling and your mission, not part of someone else's agenda.**

The fact is, people exploit a Christian Nice Guy's naïveté and passivity. Some bosses and peers know that a fearful disposition makes you easier to manipulate—it may even be one reason you were hired. Such people will saddle you with *their* responsibilities, and they will do so with remarkable cleverness. They'll set you up in meetings, corner you in hallways, and spring information on you that they had long ago but find it to their advantage to withhold so they can later put you on the spot.

Certain co-workers, not exactly altar boys, know that because you don't like conflict or unresolved problems, you're prone to make decisions too quickly, so they'll demand a quick answer from you, even when it's not necessary. *Here's what every Christian Nice Guy needs to memorize for such situations: "I'll get back with you on that."* If pushed for a specific time, don't be too specific; do say you'll check your schedule, and don't talk on and on (another CNG weakness). Shoot back a few questions of your own, like, "How long have you known about this (problem, need, whatever it is)?" Often, he who owns the questions owns the conversation; questions are your friends, part of the armor of workplace self-protection. As Jesus exemplifies, there's no sin whatsoever in protecting yourself from the hidden agendas and entrapping inquiries of others.

As a result of their blindness to workplace deceit, CNGs end up with wool pulled over their eyes. Even when they recognize that they're being told half-truths (the hardest ones to spot in the workplace), they so viscerally fear conflict that if they confront they don't know how to do so with tact, which further damages their careers. Or they ignore the offense, which may help them get along with their co-workers, but not with their wives and children, whom they promised to protect and for whom they pledged to provide. *By hiding from conflict, Christian Nice Guys break their sacred vows before God; a CNG lives a sinful lifestyle.*

He desperately wants to find a way around this. Similar to the sentiment of the infamous (and naïve) Rodney King, he screams inside, "Can't we all just get along?!" The answer, brother, is no. A purposeful life includes conflict, and there is no other path, not in this lifetime. Just know that redemptive conflict will feel and become more natural, and you'll see and realize its results—please keep reading.

> **By hiding from conflict, Christian Nice Guys break their sacred vows before God; a CNG lives a sinful lifestyle.**

Don't let the fate of Ken, a CNG from Texas, be yours as well: "For years I was stuck in menial low-paying jobs, hoping to advance, while others got promoted over me. Then when I did get a promotion eight years later, I became so afraid of losing the position that I became a people pleaser and others walked all over me. I lost that job." Elliot, a CNG from Kansas, knows that he's in a dead-end job: "I'd rather be doing something else, but I don't have the confidence to leave that comfort zone. People walk all over me." Neither of these men are good providers.

YOUR BOSS AS YOUR "COVERING"?

Have you ever been told that your boss is part of your biblical "covering"? Whether yes or no, I have discovered that the meaning of this "covering" is left to the boss's interpretation. Makes sense, too, because you won't find this idea conclusively represented in the Bible; it's a modern-day church fabrication, and guess who it benefits?

I had a boss tell me and my co-workers during workplace "Bible studies" about his covering in our lives. Wouldn't you know it, many if not most of those studies ended with admonishments to obey the authority figures in our life, to work hard as working unto the Lord, and related directives. They were good and right messages, but they were hollow and self-serving coming from him. Oh, the madness we CNGs have tolerated in the name of being nice Christians.

Again, since this supposed covering is an extra-biblical revelation, the person who speaks it into being gets to define what it means. My boss, whom I should not have mistaken as a leader, told me that I was to put myself under his teaching the same way I was supposed to follow and not question my pastor. He was part of the biblical authority structure in my life now, and if I didn't obey him, then he might withhold his "blessing" in my life the way God, he said, withholds his blessing from those who disobey.

Such teaching was in line with the doctrine put forward by the heavy-handed church I attended at the time. I "submitted" myself to his authority, and my, the stories I could tell.

I eventually wised up and found another job. (Nice Guys: Don't tell people you're looking for another job. Just do it, and not because you're afraid of being fired, but because you want to preserve your integrity.) When I told my boss, he said he was withholding his God-powered blessing. The words I then uttered aided my climb out of the CNG hole: "I don't want your 'blessing.' It doesn't exist."

Christian Nice Guys are fodder for such manipulation; they *need* the strong people in our churches to defend them against this nonsense, because this isn't even close to the worst of such ideas. Some CNGs even come to believe that not only are they to seek their boss's "blessing," they are to identify themselves with actual slavery, a kiss of death for a passive person. This is the message of one of the bestselling authors ever of books for Christian men, a man who has helped other men in many ways, but not in this one important area. He inserts two words into Scripture to give his ideas some glue: "Slaves [employees], obey your earthly masters [employers] in everything" (Colossians 3:22).

This influential man is saying that an employee's labors or services are similar to that obtained through force, that their physical beings are regarded as the property of another person, and that employees are entirely subject to their boss's/owner's will. Christian men have been told to identify themselves with slaves, who, for the most part, since earliest times, have been legally defined as *things;* therefore, they could be bought, sold, traded, gifted, or pledged for a debt by their owner. The church's message to men in this regard is abysmal: You are the plaything of others, unworthy of the dignity that's intrinsic to being made in God's image. That's one of the main reasons Christians fought to end slavery in the first place!

This same popular author says we're to serve our earthly boss because "he holds God's proxy as our employer." Basically, employers are God's substitutes, his stand-ins, so to speak. What a monstrously abusive, potentially absurd, possibly heretical concept. What if your boss is a crook—is God now crooked? Taking comparisons and analogies too far has been a tragic church specialty in regard to the lives of men for too long.

I understand part of what this otherwise helpful man is trying to say: Our work should be a good testimony regardless of our circumstances. We're to work hard and be honest in all our endeavors, even when our good behavior is not reciprocated. Nevertheless, this doesn't mean you are anything close to a slave—that would mean you have no choices. Don't *ever* believe you don't have choices. That's an evil lie.

Your workplace loyalty is to God and to the gifts he's given you. And if you're married, your loyalties also include your wife, and kids if you have them. You never swore an allegiance to your boss, and you were never required to do so; just don't put it past the male-diminishing church to try to create one.

> **Don't *ever* believe you don't have choices. That's an evil lie.**

Fatherless boys, or boys who grew up with an "absent" father, have become easy prey for spiritual abuse and predatory motives of other men in the workplace who sense their lack of perceived masculinity. In sharp contrast, God says we shouldn't take advantage of the fatherless (Exodus 22:22) and that true religion looks after the fatherless (James 1:27). It's time for the church to flex some real muscle on behalf of the weak and the needy.

FINAL WORKPLACE WARNING

It is often folly to try to change your workplace environment—such change is usually out of your control, and you'll likely waste huge amounts of energy while bringing about no substantive difference. I know. It was, in part, workplace injustice that motivated me to write this book. Instead, though, I turned my complaining into what I call "blessed dissatisfaction." I took that pain, frustration, and anger and charted a new and proactive course.

A study in 2004 confirmed that bad work environments can get your creative juices flowing like few other experiences: It said that some of the best ideas and creative results can rise from the blues in the workplace. Many meaningful endeavors have been launched while in the throes of vocational pain, and many worthy undertakings wouldn't have been launched if it weren't for the thorny ground of difficulty. Take comfort from this; good *can* and does come from bad.

Nevertheless also be wise. Robert Kennedy warned, "Progress is a nice word. But change is its motivator. And change has its enemies."

In order to chart a better work life, I stopped playing defense all the time. I came out of my bunker, because the essence of what General Douglas MacArthur said is right: All defense and no offense gets you nowhere. *Niceness is both an excuse and a euphemism for mediocrity.*

And don't take this as an excuse to be needlessly irresponsible. "Take calculated risks," advised General George Patton. "That is quite different from being rash."

If this describes you, your new course could mean changing jobs and working in a place where people are more or less respected on a daily basis. But again, don't expect perfection: Don't let a good workplace fall prey to immature notions of perfection. Remember, there is no Job Charming. No one gets out of the workplace unscathed by sin, their own and/or someone else's.

I believe in sacrifice in the workplace—just make sure it's a real sacrifice. Here's what I mean: *It's a virtue to lay down your rights for the love of another. It's foolish and destructive to lay down your rights in the workplace because you fear what will happen if you don't.* This is what you're doing, Nice Guys, and others see it. It's no Christian witness to be walked on because you're passive.

Being shrewd in the workplace does feel like a sin for men who grew up in churches that overemphasized gentle virtues at the expense of rugged ones. We've done our men no favors by telling them this. That they are ill-prepared for life isn't good news for employers who need wise men to conquer the high ground.

> **I believe in sacrifice in the workplace—just make sure it's a real sacrifice.**

I remember when it felt wrong to act boldly at work. I had to remind myself that it wasn't a sin for Jesus, and if it wasn't a sin for Jesus, it wasn't a sin for me either. Christian men need to think about this fact long and hard, because it's the beginning of CNG knowledge. This thought process will help you discover a core misconception: You don't think you deserve good treatment at work, and you often put a Christian veneer on it by mistaking your workplace suffering with suffering for the gospel's sake.

God has given no interoffice memo saying you are another person's property or pawn. You are your own agent, free to do in the workplace what's best for you and your family. God put a beat in you—certain abilities, desires, and attributes. Come out of your hiding place and dance to it. Act upon *that* interoffice memo.

MASCULINITY: THE JOURNEY FROM NICE GUY TO GOOD GUY (PART 1)

I'm happy tonight. I'm not worried about anything. I'm not fearing any man. Mine eyes have seen the glory of the coming of the Lord.
— DR. MARTIN LUTHER KING JR., MURDERED LESS THAN TWENTY-FOUR HOURS LATER

Life is yours to be spent. Not to be saved.
— DH LAWRENCE

Meet Snivels, the coward within me. Snivels hates it when people see him for who he really is, so he is persistently pretending and hiding. He doesn't use humor to bless others with sweet relief from their often weary days; instead, like Job in his misery, he uses humor to babble on about things far beyond him and to make small talk about wonders way over his head. Snivels does this to sap life of its uncomfortable vitality. When people laugh, he grows boastful.

Snivels is full of complaints; complaining makes him feel strong. This is why he cuts down men of action—they are the trees that keep his Coward Mill up and running—yet he offers no real alternatives. He steals the power of others, parasitically living off their verve. He knows it's easier to destroy than to create, and primarily he desires to build an aura of importance around himself.

Snivels doesn't like himself, but he's just doing what he knows—Snivels confuses life with living. He's not even sure there's a better way, because he has no philosophical guiding principles in his blood, no fixed benchmarks that could show him another path. He's simplistic; he mistakes humility for shame and thinks he's got to fix every problem he runs across in order to keep his world safe. The weight of this misconception is among his heaviest burdens.

Snivels, my coward within, loves comfort, which he thinks brings control and protection. He's terrified of conflict, so he remains silent and hopes others will mistake it for a writer's pensiveness. Instead of rescuing others from hardships by being a warrior of light, he prefers to describe the color of the water in which they drown.

Snivels recoils when my kids express deep emotion. He tempts me to hide behind a smile instead of crying and offering wise counsel. He wants me to look away when my wife is in my arms and professes abiding love. He urges me to stay indoors when it's rainy and cold, even though I have obscenely expensive gear to keep me dry and warm while fly-fishing for winter steelhead. *It's too cold, Pauly. That current's strong, isn't it? You could get pneumonia.*

Snivels loves convenience, so he's ecstatic when I hear sermons that say if I experience resistance it must be the hand of God saying no. He's elated when I try something new and give up because I mistake difficulty for God's sovereignty. That's when he uncorks the good stuff and breaks into song:

Stay where it's warm
Stay where it's safe

(Chorus)
I told you so!
I told you so!

Keep from the edges
Don't worry, Paul
Just give it up
You'll learn to love those fences
You were born for fences

There's a piece of Snivels in us all. He's at war with the better part of me and the better part of you. He's fighting masculinity, his archenemy, a God-given part of us lying under an undetermined amount of rubble. Some of the debris is from the ongoing gender war, some from misguided messages within the church, some from flat-out neglect and misunderstanding. It's time to roll away a few boulders and see what unique masculine creature comes running forth from the Christian Nice Guy tomb.

MASCULINE CONFUSION

> **Ask Christian men what it means to be masculine, which I've done as a talk show host, and they're quicker to tell you what it isn't (timid, weak, effeminate) than what it is.**

Ask Christian men what it means to be masculine, which I've done as a talk show host, and they're quicker to tell you what it isn't (timid, weak, effeminate) than what it is. There are some exceptions, but this tends to be the rule nowadays: guys in the church know more about masculinity's antonyms than its synonyms. We live in a timid age with regard to gender issues, compared to 1905, when *Webster's Dictionary* contained the following: "Masculine: Having the quality of a man; virile; not feminine or effeminate; strong; robust."

I now have one dictionary that refuses to list any tangible attributes, and this is not an oversight. Score one for the intimidation of political correctness—the war still rages. (Note also that while Christian men often know how to verbally define *masculine* or *masculinity,* they even more often have little idea of how to live it out.)

For all its strength, beauty, and virtue, the church is largely following our culture's lead regarding masculinity. Christians are confused, in part, for the reasons outlined by George Gilder:

> Surely women's liberation is a most unpromising panacea. But the movement is working [having effectiveness] politically, because our sexuality is so confused, our masculinity so uncertain, and our families so beleaguered that no one knows what they are for or how they are sustained. (*Sexual Suicide,* Introduction)

Rick Bundschuh says it this way: The church has never been "comfortable expressing the masculinity of our Lord or dwelling on the muscular side of our faith" (*Passed Thru Fire*).

SEPARATE FROM WOMEN?

We've examined much of what masculinity is not. So what *is* it? And since masculinity involves a journey, how does a man arrive at it?

The church today talks about separating men from women in order to pave the way toward masculine growth, and there's some wisdom to this.

When a player is injured in the game of soccer, the ball technically is supposed to go out of bounds before he can receive attention from anyone. Some refs uphold this rule and some don't. If I come onto the field before the referee waves me on, I can receive a warning and possibly even get kicked out of the game. I usually have to wait awhile, which gives me time to consider some common questions: *Is he moving? What part of his body is hurt? Are his parents here?*

Injury is a pivotal moment for a young man. I approach with care, but also respect, for something good can likewise happen if I get out of the way: A truth may settle. If the injury isn't "real," that is, something that doesn't cause lasting damage, something that hurts now but won't hurt so much in a few minutes, then I don't overcrowd. I don't smother with concern. This is a moment where he can learn that *pain is a part of life that has to be lived through, endured.* It's part of the journey.

He can learn that if he lets difficulty stop him, he won't get very far.

Parents and coaches (among others) sometimes short-circuit these mighty lessons by getting too close to the event. God bless them—they want to take the pain away, just as a part of me does as well.

Even so, I and the others stand back as long as we don't perceive the injury to be dire or serious. We let the event run its course, because we know there's something valuable on the other side. Men know that injuries deserve respect and praise, not fussiness. The wounded have usually done something brave to get there, and bravery warrants honor.

While helping young men handle the fear that comes from pain, I find it's best to give them space from their moms at first. Legitimate motherly concern for their sons' safety has a way of dispelling the important lessons boys need to learn if they are to embrace their masculinity. As little boys are becoming young men, the maternal desire to nurse and nurture is like a wind that can sweep away masculine growth—moms don't mean to do this, but they do.

I love the boys I coach; it's not easy for me to see them get hurt, especially when it's my own sons. My heart is not made of stone—I know what it's like. I've been knocked out three times, all on soccer fields. I once broke my leg in two places during a game. Nevertheless, my head knows something that my heart needs to obey for the good of these young men. I do not repeat the sick athletic myth that pain equals weakness. Rather, I help my boys get stronger through the pain.

> **I do not repeat the sick athletic myth that pain equals weakness. Rather, I help my boys get stronger through the pain.**

Sports can teach boys other aspects of masculinity as well. I'll have players, usually in the second half, who raise their hand for a sub. They aren't injured. They're tired. I can take them out, but there are times I'll shake my head and refuse, because I want them to learn something about themselves: They're able to endure more than they think.

A few mothers have asked me why I kept their kid in the game against his preference, and I've ended up saying many of the same words. That their son is stronger than even he realizes. That I have faith in his abilities and in his strength. That I see his strength, even when he doesn't. That I know he has what it takes, even when he doubts himself. He needs to know all of this, but he won't until he works through it himself.

The edgy culture critic Camille Paglia has said that masculinity is "achieved by a revolt from woman." This has an intellectual ring, and it likely appeals to men who've given up trying to figure out women anyway or simply harbor derogatory opinions about them. These men believe and say things like Hall-of-Famer Charles Barkley: "Listening to a woman is almost as bad as losing to one. There are only three things that women are better at than men: cleaning, cooking, and having sex." This low view of women has nothing to do with authentic masculinity.

God created woman in part to be man's "helper," his partner (Genesis 2:18). A man who loves and cherishes his woman knows that he receives from her what no one else, no other relationship, could provide. Billy Graham, for example, counts his wife, Ruth, as his most helpful advisor.

Dwight Moody's son recognized the same important dynamic in his parents' life. This innovative nineteenth-century leader left his mark on the world by going against consensus, one of the keys to his success:

> It may be safely said that in the beginning of all his greatest and most successful efforts he stood alone, acting against the advice of those best able, apparently, to judge of the matter—with the one exception of his most valued human advisor . . . his wife.

The rising contemporary movement toward the embrace of masculinity is wonderful; its prevalent emphasis on extreme separation from women for masculine growth, however, must be tempered with wisdom so as to avoid misogyny.

MASCULINITY DEFINED

Since the Bible doesn't offer a specific definition of masculinity (the word itself isn't very old), and since many within the church have provided a definition that I find troubling, I've created my own uncomplicated definition: *Biblical masculinity is guys doing what God wants guys to do, and doing it in line with their true identity—before it was marred by human sin and especially shame—leading to a virtuous life marked by redemptive creativity, protection, purpose, and love.*

This path toward masculinity isn't an overnighter, but a process that must include hope and courage while fighting through obstacles. The Christian Nice Guy needs strength around him—God as well as other trusted men and women—to help keep his confidence up. He needs values worth fighting for that will draw him into conflict in the war against truth. Encountering the opposition, he needs to press forward, facing death, if necessary, and making sure he doesn't waste his energy on life-draining complaints. When disappointment and sorrow tempt his heart to careen into places it shouldn't go, he'll need to remember his mission in order to find the blessed satisfaction I wrote about earlier. (Forming a personal mission is a CNG nonnegotiable. We'll get into this later.)

> **Biblical masculinity is guys doing what God wants guys to do, and doing it in line with their true identity—before it was marred by human sin—leading to a virtuous life marked by redemptive creativity, protection, purpose, and love.**

This masculine journey, which we see throughout the earthly life of Jesus, includes hope, faith, confidence, quest, risk, support, conviction, conflict, allegiance, few excuses, and minimum complaints.

Some Christian men know this is not where we've been headed. Says Tim, a blunt former CNG from Colorado: "We should be training our kids to be strong and confident for God. They should be the happiest, most loving, fierce, most kind, able, most willing people around. Instead, we are a bunch of wimps, generally speaking. We've turned Jesus into a wimp who performed magic tricks."

THREE TYPES OF MEN

Men should not cut compassion, gentleness, or kindness out of their personalities while on their journey into masculinity. We must, however, embrace other masculine traits, the ones Jesus showed, if our homes and society are to have the kind of men they need and if men are to live the life they were meant to live. We need to gain a better understanding of personality projections and also observe how passivity is only one of two dangerous extremes.

Passive men extend something that *looks* like grace—a disposition to be generous, helpful, and merciful. However, the reason passive men accept insults and other forms of humiliation is that they fear what might happen with an eruption of *conflict*—the sound of life happening.

They lie to their own hearts as well as the hearts of others. They hide their feelings and deny their wants and desires not because of loving sacrifice, but because they don't believe they should have them—and giving up something they never really owned is neither sacrifice nor love. Though they pride themselves on never getting angry, they harbor smoldering resentment, a kind of undisclosed anger of the mind. Their outbursts may do more damage than the actions of aggressive men, who let off steam one frustrated puff at a time.

Aggressive men are more honest—they're glad to tell you what they're thinking. However, they lack soul-warming grace, a buffer between sound and rash behavior. Aggressive men can be so quick to judge and condemn others that they fail to see the larger and more subtle issues at play and are prone to partial blindness. Accordingly, even though they are true to their feelings, what they express is dubious, just as with passive men. The real world is a tough place; it's survival of the fittest, say aggressive men, *until* they fall from their wave of strength, experience defeat, or undergo illness, when they might yearn for the mercy they themselves have rarely, if ever, given.

> **Our goal is to be like Christ, the Assertive One, who extended grace and mercy when it was warranted and spoke the stinging truth when it was called for.**

Assertive men. It's this type we must seek to be. Our goal is to be like Christ, the Assertive One, who extended grace and mercy when it was warranted and spoke the stinging truth when it was called for. Both aggressive and passive men are simmering in the caldron of insecurity, with fears like smoldering logs beneath. *Their fears will keep burning until they are confronted.*

You'll see these three personality types and their weaknesses on the popular television show *American Idol.* Passive Paula Abdul is gracious, but often not truthful. Aggressive Simon Cowell is truthful, but often not gracious. Then there's the assertive Randy Jackson, who is good (but not perfect) at mixing grace with truth, making his criticism fruitful as opposed to just painful. His words contain encouragement and instruction even though they're not immune to disapproval. *You'll* be booed too, once you decide to be truthful. (Whether or not you call people "dawg" is up to you.)

CHRISTIAN BOLDNESS VS. WORLDLY CONFLICT

Nice Guys often have a flawed understanding of conflict because as kids they were exposed to the fire-breathing kind that batters and doesn't lead to fruitful resolution. There's good conflict as well; CNGs need to recognize both.

First, though, note this fundamental Nice Guy misunderstanding: They think the opposite of conflict is appeasement, which sometimes includes timid deception. The opposite of conflict actually is resolution, a process that demands bold truthfulness.

Also, not all boldness is Christian boldness, which, according to Paul's words for the once-timorous Timothy, is defined by "power, love, and a sound mind," including common sense (2 Timothy 1:7 NKJV).

I saw both worldly conflict and Christian boldness as KDOV program director. I was sometimes privy to how popular church leaders lived during the week. I saw quickly that you couldn't last long in ministry if you thought you had to be nice all the time; tough decisions must be made, and the best leaders followed Paul's prescription to Timothy. They operated from these core attributes, which kept them and their congregations on course. They minimized unnecessary suffering from hard feelings, because wherever two or more are gathered, there is opinion. Though we all hold our opinions dear, a hard fact of life is that all opinions are not created equal. Someone has to make a final call, or else a church will flounder.

I also saw others who drove hard and even deceptive bargains. They operated from fear, which they covered up. They were sweet and smiley from the pulpit on the weekends, and then they sliced and diced people during the week. Their style of conflict was as worldly as any fleshly CEO.

Their two-faced approach toward conflict had deeper ramifications: They would encourage the men in their congregations to be amiable Christian Nice Guys while they themselves followed an aggressive course behind the scenes. They were actors, well versed in the art of dissimulation. And it got them places—their will was done.

Thus, the CNG would draw a deadly comparison: *Look at him—look how effective he is in life. So nice, yet so dynamic. That's how life should be lived. I need to be more like him.* Left holding the bag, again. False testimonies are a tyranny in the lives of Christian Nice Guys too naïve to spot deception.

CNGs are afraid to be bold, because the church has them petrified of sin. They're afraid that when they move into masculinity they may misstep, say something wrong, upset the order of things. They worry that they may go overboard and not behave perfectly. *If I live small, I'll sin less.*

By now you can see that living small is profoundly sinful: Peace that avoids and denies actual conflict is counterfeit, using passivity as an excuse. When you're tempted to fall back into that destructive way of thinking, remember the words of Martin Luther: If you're going to sin, he said, then you ought to "sin boldly." That's as forgivable as your current timid sin, so what are you worried about?

> **Living small is profoundly sinful: Peace that avoids and denies actual conflict is counterfeit, using passivity as an excuse.**

I hear people testify in church that they know they are making the right decisions in life because they "feel God's peace." Conversely, many times when I've followed what God says in his Word, I feel turmoil. I've never stood up for justice, for example, without getting pounded by someone and then licking deep wounds; at the same time, I know that my actions have brought my Lord pleasure and, hopefully, glory—*this* brings a peace that surpasses understanding. Christian living is not a series of unbroken feel-good moments. That's New Age mumbo-jumbo.

It's time to be more (not less) offensive while standing up for truth. It's time to give people what my friend Dr. Kevin Leman calls Vitamin N: "Tell people no. It's good for you and others." Charles Spurgeon likewise advised his students, "Learn to say no. It will do you more good than Latin."

The Bible says that "the righteous are as bold as a lion" (Proverbs 28:1). It's safe to say we are not yet remarkably bold. Let's give people some Vitamin B—boldness—because it's good for our souls and for theirs.

BESTOWED FROM MEN TO MEN

Nice Guys tend to have compliant fathers, making it especially difficult for them to break free. My father was often quiet and unavailable during key periods of my youth.

In the last year of his life, however, he gave me a gift I didn't know I wanted and to some degree didn't know I needed in order to live a less-encumbered, more purposeful, life. He told me he thought I had what it takes to make it in life, a sentiment he'd never before shared in words. Robert Bly, now a grandfather of the contemporary men's movement, calls this act the giving of "my name," meaning that *my father affirmed my masculine lineage.* His blessing came a little late—after a mortgage, wife, three kids, and the toll of typical adult struggles—but hey, it came! More important, he told me and showed me that he was in my corner. He cheered me on. My spirit soared to heights I didn't think possible, and I've been freer since that unexpected blessing.

It's vital that we fathers do the same with our sons, and also with our daughters. I emphasize boys here because emotionally disturbed boys out-number girls four to one, and I don't need some white-haired sociologist from Sweden to tell me why. I've seen it: Boys feel alone out there. When the essential question *Do I have what it takes?* isn't affirmed by another man, guys are left to wander and to wonder. Though they may appear confident, many question their own abilities to provide for and protect a family, to the point of ulcers or hypertension.

I know that some men will never receive this blessing from their biological father. I almost didn't. This is why Christian Nice Guys should pursue a relationship with at least one man who can help them obtain greater masculinity. Caution: Here's where CNGs are likely to make a significant error: They are prone to pick out another CNG, someone even farther along the road of niceness and passive-aggression than they! Broaden your definition of masculinity to include men who embrace life's rugged side—

I don't need some white-haired sociologist from Sweden to tell me why. I've seen it: Boys feel alone out there.

that's the grafting you need. Pick a man who's bold, the way Jesus was. A man who knows that life shouldn't be lived with a faked wink and a forced smile.

MASCULINITY IS SPELLED P-R-O-A-C-T-I-V-E

I cannot overstress the importance of beginning the great work of being proactive rather than reactive in life. Writes Dale Carnegie: "Inaction breeds doubt and fear. Action breeds confidence and courage. If you want to conquer fear, do not sit home and think about it. Go out and get busy."

Proactivity is penicillin to your Nice Guy infection. Here's why: CNGs spend a lot of time counterpunching, which wastes precious emotional and physical reserves. Accept these facts: Life is a difficult battle, demanding conflict and struggle. The best way to meet this requirement is by taking the battle to life, not letting life take the battle to you. *You'll make much more progress when you're offensive.* True, it won't be easy, but think about the wisdom and practicality of this: You'll be giving the same amount of output you did when you lived reactively, only soon you'll be thriving instead of just surviving.

Also, being proactive is a kind of mosquito repellant: it keeps the bloodsuckers away. Nice Guys, you do have bloodsuckers in your life, people who sense your deficiencies and use them against you. This is the answer to a question that haunts you: *Why do people feel so comfortable picking on me?* Because they know they can. You transmit a discernable deficiency, and the predators know it. They can smell your weakness. They aren't about to change any time soon, so don't waste your time trying to rehabilitate them. Predators listen to people with a bigger stick, and your stick isn't very big—yet.

> **We cannot fulfill Christ's requirement for wisdom, shrewdness, or cunning unless we are proactive.**

Proactivity is a learned discipline that brings improved harmony in your life as you go deeper and deeper into this reality of the masculine. And something that people might mistake for magic happens when you maintain this discipline. Opportunity calls, often in seemingly mysterious ways. Johann Wolfgang von Goethe, playwright, poet, and novelist, knew what he was talking about when he wrote of the unique happenings that stem from living proactively.

> Until one is committed, there is hesitancy, the chance to draw back, always ineffectiveness. Concerning all acts of initiative and creation, there is one elementary truth the ignorance of which kills countless ideas and splendid plans: that the moment one definitely commits oneself, then providence moves too. All sorts of things occur to help one that would never otherwise have occurred. A whole stream of events issues from the decision, raising in one's favor all manner of unforeseen incidents, meetings and material assistance which no man could have dreamed would have come his way. Whatever you can do or dream you can, begin it. Boldness has genius, power . . . in it. Begin it now.

We cannot fulfill Christ's requirement for wisdom, shrewdness, or cunning unless we are proactive; these are active, forward-moving behaviors. The road to holiness is paved by what we do as well as what we don't do. Proactivity is doing what we know we should be doing, and it's good for our bodies as well; says David, "When I kept silent, my bones wasted away" (Psalm 32:3).

When you immerse yourself into masculinity, become submerged in it, you begin to take on its qualities. And there's a desire in you for masculinity, an innate recognition that your maleness is good; at the same time, something in you also knows that masculinity will be disruptive to your current life. That's when the Snivels within, the coward who wants to call the shots, rears his ugly head and tries to take over. Our culture is partial to Snivels; don't expect society to help you put him under wraps. The church in general is somewhat duped by Snivels as well—it's much harder to spot the sin of inaction than almost any sins of action—so use caution there too.

You beat Snivels down by being proactive, by consistently choosing to take on challenges that make you want to step back. Start with smaller ones, then work up from there. You'll become a different guy when you do this regularly, and, speaking of regularity, the life of a Christian man gives him plenty of opportunities for such improvement. If a situation makes you uncomfortable, chances are it's a great place to show Snivels who's really the boss. God didn't give you the spirit of Snivelish timidity; welcome his spirit of boldness instead. Passivity will become merely a temptation to sin instead of a sinful and dishonest lifestyle.

More great news is that masculinity is also a discipline, not some mystical energy force "out there," deciphered by a select few while the rest of us are kept in the cold. The next chapter describes more of this attainable quality.

MASCULINITY: THE JOURNEY FROM NICE GUY TO GOOD GUY (PART 2)

For young boys, if they feel they don't have the right stuff, they learn to live with the right bluff.

— JOE EHRMANN, FORMER NFL STAR AND COACH

The most accurate standard for judging people's attachment to G–d is the extent to which they hate evil and fight against those who oppress the innocent.

— RABBI SHMULEY BOTEACH

s we've seen, masculinity compels a man into areas of risk that he otherwise might not enter. This driving force that *can* be perverted by shame is the very power that *will* help transform passive Nice Guys into proactive Good Guys—if they'll persist past all the false expectations that hound them.

Contrary to what we've heard in church and seen on television, *masculinity is best nurtured by what is truly feminine and domestic;* true domesticity protects those in a man's kingdom with heart and mind; domesticity blesses others with real help, rather than that which merely alleviates discomfort;

domesticity embraces righteous anger, a motor toward better living for a man and those he loves; and domesticity sees the world as it really is, to the betterment of all.

IN PRAISE OF DOMESTICITY

Earlier I outlined problems with the over-domestication of men. Now it's time to sing domestication's praises, for healthy doses of it *feed* masculinity. Men, if they're wise, want some degree of domestic life because it is designed to improve them; domestic life gives us a venue for spiritual growth that's unlike many other settings. For example, if you're a selfish man, it *will* become apparent in a home. If you're passive, this too will become obvious.

Most of us don't want to feel like drifters forever anyway. There's a time for desert wandering and testing, and there's a time to seek God-designed shelter from this harsh world.

I remember my single-guy nomad days; all those roommates, the not-so-pleasant smells,

> **Masculinity is best nurtured by what is truly feminine and domestic.**

the ugly utilitarian sights, and the feeling that *there has to be more to life than this*! I wanted to put down roots, but I sure wasn't going to spend that kind of energy on those guys. I cared about them; don't get me wrong—I even loved some of them. But I longed for a group I could call my own. Only then would I sacrifice for the want of this rooted desire. The lack of fulfillment that accompanies living with other men pushed me into the arms of domestic life and to commit the sacrifice required to deserve it.

So now, fifteen years later, usually during movie nights at home, I survey our darkened living room and take inventory of this small, five-person colony of mine. Limbs dangle from couches and overstuffed chairs. Someone's grousing for a back rub, scalp massage, a glass of cold water. Someone throws out an observation about what just happened in the film, and the rest of us weigh it in our minds. Sometimes the responses I hear are funny and wise. Our kids are learning to make such comments *between* dramatic moments so they don't get shushed.

I know this domestic creation will end. They will leave this home and usher in an indelible change. They will depart, if not in prosperity and opportunity, then in folly or (God forbid) tragedy. Nothing stays the same. There's no instant replay during these winsome moments; you have to savor them as they're fed to you because you can't reheat them. I sense that these rich moments, which grow and end at the same time, are the better portions of life. During these times, when I'm at my best, I sacrifice a part of myself so some love will settle in—hope and faith too. When my wife and three children need these gifts, they'll find them giving ballast to their lives much like the great hand of God.

These limbs lying leisurely along with mine are connected to my children, flesh of my flesh, destined to struggle with my judgments that are usually just and sometimes petty. When the natural blinders of youth fall from their eyes, they will see me for who I really was as a father. Make no mistake about it, we raise our own biographers. I hope my love for them covers my mistakes. I'm banking on it. We don't have a choice as parents, or as children of God.

Thomas Jefferson, Mr. Accomplishment, counted being in the warm bosom of his family among his greatest moments in life. I have felt the warmth of my family's bosom as well. Like no other experience, it fuels an engine somewhere in my chest. Their innocent goodwill has rehabilitated my broken heart. Their tenderness grows me as a man. Genuine love grows masculinity.

Then I think about what young men see on the pro wrestling channel (or whatever it's called). I call it the Raw Sewage Channel: men pretending to beat each other to a pulp for vanity's sake—and for money—not for the protection of what is good, beautiful, and right. That's male energy gone bad, and boys with holes in their masculine hearts can't spot the counterfeit. I'm told Christians are in that profession. That's like saying you're a Christian photographer with *Playboy*. Time to repent, and change jobs.

Domestication, which at its best is the demonstration of love, is good for men as long as we aren't required to live by a purely feminine understanding of it. We must make room for a melding of both feminine and masculine definitions of what it means to love and what love in a home looks like.

Male domestic love is often not demonstrated through sentimental actions; Emerson Eggerichs points out that Jesus' loving actions rarely fell on the sentimental side. We guys are inclined to give physical and tangible acts of love.

For instance, I replaced a sewer line behind one of my homes. I saw and smelled things I wish I'd never encountered. Another time, with a freshly separated shoulder, I replaced a sump pump. The pain was incredible.

I spent hours under one house putting up insulation—exhausting work with only inches of clearance. I lay for hours in cold water, wearing a coverall so small it cut into my groin. It was dark, gloomy, and sometimes creepy. I lost orientation after a while. My mind played tricks on me, and in my goggles and mask I felt like I was scuba diving on land.

I felt good after doing all of these projects and more. I endured discomfort for my family's betterment. It was my way of saying, "I love you guys." However, this isn't a commonly accepted definition. When a guy gets up on the roof and fixes a leak or goes out in a rainstorm and unclogs a downspout, we don't call it love. Such sacrifice is not granted the nobility it deserves.

This isn't the only way we guys should show love. We show love to those with whom we share our hearts—*communication connects us*; so guys, let's keep talking. Ladies, be good stewards with your power of words, and count on us to connect with you verbally, but know that repairing and fixing (for example) is a way for us to give love too. Many of us guys consider such labors far superior to sentimental expressions like flowers or chocolates; we'd sometimes rather do something for you than give you perishable gifts.

Ironically, some of the most manipulative men I've ever known have been big gift givers. When they mess up at home, they bring flowers. How sweet—really shows how brokenhearted he is, doesn't it? He stops for five minutes on the way home, slaps down a little cash while yakking on his cell phone, then shows up with a few blooms, and *poof!* instant happiness and marital bliss? No. Ladies, sometimes that's far more of an insult than an apology or restitution.

MASCULINITY PROTECTS THE WEAK

Domesticity fostering masculinity should become an umbrella that protects the weak more than it protects us. Recently one of my boys didn't make a sports team. The news was delivered bluntly, deeply injuring his spirit. I've been in his shoes, so I was familiar with the litany of words to come, the same ones I put forth like a lawyer more than twenty years ago. He couldn't understand why he didn't make it—a handful of less-talented kids did. The world was no longer as it appeared; injustice had slapped him, and the realization spun his mind into anger.

I tried to comfort him. He allowed some hugs, refused others. He laughed, but cried more. He hit a wall. He wanted to go out with Mom to do some light shopping. He said the following statements within ten seconds of each other, I kid you not: "It doesn't matter, Dad, it really doesn't. . . . They're idiots! They made a mistake!" His mind was reeling, and his words didn't make much sense.

I tried to console him again. I repeated a familiar story, how I didn't make the varsity soccer team as a sophomore, and I knew I had better skills than most that weren't cut. That was true, but there was another truth I didn't want to admit: I was smaller than most as well. Varsity ball would have crushed me. Fuming and embarrassed, I set out to prove the world wrong. I was captain of the junior varsity team. I knew more about the game than our coach. Regularly I practiced on my own, working on the weak side of my game. I was a varsity captain the next year. I set a school record. He knows the story. He's heard it before. It helped, but not much this time.

I told him it wasn't a good idea for him to go out with Mom on that pivotal night, that it would be wise to stay home, that home is a good place to be when you're in pain. He said I was wrong—then in the same breath, said yes; yes, I was right. Then he broke down, cried some more, and ran to his room.

My heart broke for my boy. He asked me to contact his coach to find out why he didn't make the team. He didn't have to ask me twice. I had his back. I wanted to know too.

Only one thing would bring relief to him that night: He loves to pluck rogue hairs off my back. Sounds gross, I know, but it is what it is. So I took my shirt off, put a pillow under my stomach, and let him rip. He inspected like a treasure hunter looking for clues. I heard him laugh. A smile returned to his voice. My hurt was offset by the lift in his mood, and he went to bed with some salve on his wounds. Domesticity had stitched him up along with a crafty desire to outwit his pain, a hallmark of authentic masculinity.

I once worked with a man who repaired planes on an aircraft carrier. He spent most of his time repairing leaky hydraulic systems and was sometimes forced to ground "birds" against the will of their pilots. He said he had no choice—it was his job to hold on to the planes until they were ready to fly again.

I look at parenting through similar eyes. It's my job to help my kids fly well, and occasionally this means keeping them away from the world for a spell, usually one long and mercurial night. There's a time to be a homebody and seek refuge in a board game, or in a TV show, or in plucking unsightly hairs from your old man's back.

Home is a place to salve our miseries, to lay low while pain, a powerful and hated minister, searches for ways to get at us. When it comes to kids, timing is everything, so sometimes we need to tell it: *Not tonight. You can mold him tomorrow, but tonight he's mine.* Telling our children's angry disappointments to get lost for the night is like applying the Lamb's blood to our doorposts at Passover; this way they will know that God's mercies are new every morning, and that we're fully on their side also. They need time to regroup and to handle life's necessary suffering with strength they wouldn't have otherwise—and they can, thanks to this spectacular creation called home, where masculine energy should be free to pulse and protect.

Telling our children's angry disappointments to get lost for the night is like applying the Lamb's blood to our doorposts at Passover; this way they will know that God's mercies are new every morning, and that we're fully on their side also.

Sadly, too many men take this masculine frontier lightly, because, as shown earlier, they aren't allowed to define what it means. They feel limited and unappreciated. They miss out on tremendous blessings and on the opportunity to bless others. As George Santayana said, this wonderful world can be hard for a man to spot initially: "It takes patience to appreciate domestic bliss." Volatile men, those who have not learned to harness their fear and pain, don't see the value in home life and thereby come to "prefer unhappiness."

I've seen too many kids suffer for this vacuum of domestic/masculine protection; Nice Guys had that void also. But I have great news: *You didn't have to get it then to give it now, so let's kick evil in the teeth, men, and create more of this blessing today.*

USE WORDS THAT PROTECT AND AFFIRM

Words of affirmation, like *strong, brave, talented,* and *valuable,* are indescribably important for our boys. These words, especially when combined with words that protect, say that you are completely behind your kids. Learn to back up your words with actions, and your children will believe what they're told.

My father wasn't always passive. He did speak up and act; I just wished he'd done more of it during key times at home in my young life. I recall one vacation where I was allowed to get dirty from head to toe. All day long! Covered in hallowed mud!

I remember walking back to our trailer alongside my dad when a nearby woman offered her two cents: "If that was my son," she said in a voice like a sick crow, "I'd fan his annie!" I didn't know what an annie was—I had to ask my dad—but I knew I didn't want any part of my body fanned by her.

"Well, isn't he lucky he's not your son?" Dad said quickly in his lyrical Irish accent and with perfect comedic timing. He wasn't prone to such direct talk, so I feasted on every syllable. I stared at that mean lady with the smuggest look I could muster: *Well, looky here! See who I have in my corner?*

He told me, "There's nothing wrong with you, Paul. But there's something wrong with her." He didn't try to fix her. He didn't explain the need for a boy to get dirty sometimes; he knew it would be like talking to the breeze. All wisdom began and ended with my father on that warm and muddy evening, and I couldn't have been more proud. Or secure. I had a lion behind me in this scary world that loves to prey on little boys. He lobbed blessed sarcasm at that old biddy, the kind Jesus deployed on my behalf as well.

Words also destroy, as I clearly saw in the life of a high school friend. I and my buddies would go to his house to pick him up, and sometimes his father, a short man, would greet us, often washing his muscle car, clearly an extension of the image he wanted the world to regard.

"Why do you guys want to hang around that wussy?!" he'd yell in an alpha male voice.

We'd give him a nervous laugh with big smiles, as if what he said was actually funny. We didn't know what to say to a father who so degraded his son's identity. He said it as if he were joking, and perhaps to him he was, but I didn't see good-natured humor in my friend's response. I saw disquietude in his young eyes and lowness in his countenance; though he was accustomed to the cruel jabs, I saw a part of him die when they landed.

He wasn't sure about his masculinity, and so, like many other young men, he adopted our culture's messed-up view of masculinity. He adopted the trappings of machismo and surrounded himself with the paraphernalia of bravado: big truck, guns, indiscriminate swearing, tobacco, pot, beer. He admired pro wrestlers (he thought it was real) and spewed tales of sexual exploits. All of this, what experts call *"compensatory masculinity,"* is what boys embrace and do when they don't receive regular love, discipline, and modeling from a good father.

> **"Compensatory masculinity" is what boys embrace and do when they don't receive regular love, discipline, and modeling from a good father.**

However, the young men around him knew he was pretending, and they (including me) mocked him behind his back. The hole in him was a father hole; his dad was a weak man pretending to be strong, a man whose wife seemed to disappear before your eyes as he drained her of power. Weak people, the Snivels of the world, always exhaust others.

My friend needed paternal words of affirmation, but instead got a veiled enemy who fired lies about his manhood like bullets through his lungs. We're not robots. That bitter treatment will harvest masculinity the way hunters harvest deer.

GOOD VS. NICE

Acquiring greater masculinity means we gain greater insight into what it means to be good. Nice Guys enable; for instance, they pay the rent for someone who doesn't work, not because he's disabled but because he makes himself unemployable through drugs, alcohol, or out-of-control rampages. Good Guys allow others to suffer when it's necessary, with the desire and prayer that they'll face their difficulties in life and, through them, will grow and mature. Good people provide encouragement and support to do the right thing instead of helping people continue to do the wrong thing. Nice people try to fix others; good people tell others that it's up to them to make their lives better and that surrendering to God is the best choice they can make.

Nice drug and alcohol treatment programs would let addicts keep using and abusing drugs and people; they'd tell desperate souls that "everything will be okay" when there was no true reason to believe it. Good treatment programs confront people with the truth of their lives so they can be set free. Nice people put Band-Aids on gaping life wounds; good people perform confrontational heart-saving surgery.

Good people put their pain to good use for others, as did crime crusader John Walsh, whose son, Adam, was abducted in 1981 and later murdered. A CNG would have suffered mostly in silence and made sure not to get angry in public out of belief that being mild is a virtue even in response to faith-stealing injustice. But Walsh isn't a Nice Guy. He harnessed his anguish and created a crime-fighting network that so far has helped capture hundreds of criminals on the run, including fifteen on the FBI's Most Wanted list.

Then there's John Rabe, a German businessman who helped stop the murder of up to 250,000 Chinese civilians at the hands of the Japanese during World War II; he has been called the Oskar Schindler of China and is the subject of the outstanding book *The Good Man of Nanking*. But while everyone seemingly knows about Paris Hilton's wardrobe choices or one of the Olson twins' eating disorder, they've never heard about Rabe's courage. One day he saw a Chinese girl being raped by numerous armed Japanese soldiers. Furious, he beat them soundly and then threw them out of the room, armed with nothing but righteous anger and a booming voice. By default, Christians are taught to judge Rabe more on his insufficient display of piety (*Did he swear when he manhandled those animals? And true Christians don't use physical violence, Mr. Rabe.*) than admire and endorse his inspiring bravery.

I have worked side by side with some of my state's most powerful and philanthropic businesspeople. Not one of them should be characterized as being merely nice—they have too much backbone to be described as pleasant and agreeable all the time. They are purpose-oriented, and though their purposes involve self-interest, they also give generously to charity. Effective, successful, giving (that is, *good*) people do not feel compelled to constantly project "nice." The Bible and the chronicles of history are full of countless such examples.

GETTING BACK OUR OUTRAGE

William Bennett wrote a relevant book, *The Death of Outrage*, that asks an excellent question: What has happened to our ability to be outraged? He and many others within the church see too little of it.

I don't claim to know all the answers for this, but I do know one unreported reason: In today's evangelical subculture, Christians, especially Christian men, aren't supposed to get angry about anything. See where this leaves us? Though it's true that avoiding anger governs our ability to do damage, it also limits our ability to do good. Furthermore, our sidestepping of anger is usually more about ignoring the reality of a situation (rather than our choosing at a given time to be unexpressive); eventually, if left unaddressed, the inner anger will simply blow out of us in some other form or venue.

> **Though it's true that avoiding anger governs our ability to do damage, it also limits our ability to do good.**

Anger itself is neither good nor bad. Remember what Paul wrote? *"Be angry and do not sin"* (Ephesians 4:26 ESV). Anger's rightness depends on the direction we move with its power and energy. By and large, though, Christians don't believe anger is a legitimate power source; they fail to see it as an engine for righteous indignation that helps us confront the problems hurting our fellowman. By shunning all expressions of anger, we reduce our ability to be forces for redemption.

If we read a newspaper on any given day, we should find a lot to be angry about, like when I read how sinister entrepreneurs were selling a video on which they incited homeless people to fight one another while cameras rolled. These predators were making money by getting some of the most beleaguered people in society to pummel one another. Staring at a homeless man showing the camera his bloody tooth, my heart filled with anger; I growled and I sweated. Normally, we look away, and when we *do* speak about such horrible behavior, we often dismiss it as being some expected part of the "end times," as if this makes it all disappear or become irrelevant. Anger can be a stimulant, a motivator to propel our indifferent hearts into redemptive action.

A person with a sincere attachment to God, says Rabbi Shmuley Boteach, "will manifest his or her faith in loathing cruelty and abhorring mercilessness. Those who are detached from G–d are usually fearful in the face of evil."

Ignoring anger not only makes men less likely to do good, it leaves some depressed. Writes Jonathon Heide of *New Man* magazine:

> Psychologist David Decker works with men who never said a mean word to anyone. These men are so conditioned to dismiss their feelings of anger, they don't even know how to get mad. Some of these men live out the standard male expectation . . . but feel no human connection, in part because they don't deal with emotions, including anger. For Christian men, the pressure to contain themselves seems even tighter.

Some guys at the Men's Center, a counseling organization in Minneapolis, live there because keeping their anger inside has caused them to turn off their emotions altogether. Wives bring their husbands because they "can't get a reaction out of him" and because "he just tells me whatever he thinks I want to hear." It's safe to say that the Men's Center is full of CNGs: emotionally vacant, full of repressed anger that someday may erupt into slaying rage, recipients of bad advice, owners of stifled personalities.

How does this bring glory to God? *Especially* when considering that anger, properly directed, brings glory to God? The wrath of men shall praise you, says the Bible (Psalm 76:10), and the fear of the Lord is to hate evil (Proverbs 8:13). Right now, Christian Nice Guys hate only what disrupts comfort. Something has to change; we need to repent of this disguised vice if we're to have a real relationship with God.

I interviewed the late youth minister Mike Yaconelli numerous times before his sudden death, and once he told me about meeting Mother Teresa. "She's tough as nails, Paul. She's uncompromising and she irritates people. She's willful and domineering. She gets angry. She's not nice, but no one would say she isn't good." *Sounds like the authentic Jesus of the Gospels.*

Here's one example of anger being an engine for good. My friend's daughter was in a car wreck and almost died. She was paralyzed and needing special care, so he moved away for a while to be close to her and help with her grueling physical therapy. His main relief from the stressful situation was to ride his road bicycle, something he and I do a lot together.

But wouldn't you know it, someone took bolt cutters, cut his chain, and stole the bike from a secure area. I was *furious,* and I wasn't going to let this stand. I called up a bunch of friends; we pooled our money, and we helped him buy a better bicycle than he had before. *Take that!* I shouted in my mind. Anger propelled me and others to do a good thing we wouldn't have done if we'd followed the CNG script to never get angry.

Anger is an expression of our will, which brings Christian Nice Guys to another dilemma: They worry that expressing their will may lead them into sin, so they opt once again for life-crippling inaction. So whose will should we follow? Ours or God's?

Let me suggest that it's both. The more you conform to Christ's teaching and example, the more godly you'll become and the more you'll adopt God's will for your life. Even so, this isn't magic—you don't just sit there and (poof!) it happens. It's an active pursuit as you play a role in your own life: "A man's ways are before the eyes of the Lord, and he [the Lord] makes level all his [a man's] paths" (Proverbs 5:21 ESV). I see this as a dual nature of life: God and you working together to actualize the power of loving redemption in this fallen world. There's nothing passive or sinful about your will when it's in line with his.

MASCULINITY SEES THE WORLD CLEARLY

There's an essential toughness that's intrinsic to real masculinity; part of this is understanding how the world really operates, since it's no virtue to be ignorant of such things. That goes to the heart of the CNG problem:

The word *nice* comes from two very old and unflattering words, one French and one Latin. They both mean "ignorance, an absence of knowledge or awareness."

Ignorance of the world's ways trips up our ability to give strength for what's right. The good news is you won't find this ignorance in the human pillars of our faith. Contrary to what you've heard in church and inside your head, it's not a sin to embrace tough-minded shrewdness. In fact, it may be a sin if you don't.

> **The word *nice* comes from two very old and unflattering words, one French and one Latin. They both mean "ignorance, an absence of knowledge or awareness."**

For instance, John records how Jesus did not entrust himself to the crowds that gathered around him; he was shrewd, and he kept himself separate. We can be sure that this upset people; today, if you changed Jesus' name and told the story, we'd likely say that such a person is rude because he doesn't follow commonly accepted principles of appropriate, thoughtful social engagement (much less meet the needs and desires of others). We're taught to call such a person selfish. Christian men are supposed to try to make everyone appreciate them, even though Jesus clearly didn't do this.

As for being shrewd, I can hear the chorus of howls: *We're not supposed to know more about the world! We aren't supposed to be worldly!* But who's talking about being worldly? I'm talking about a Christian masculinity that understands how the world functions without buying into the world's destructive values.

Here's another example: Jesus, knowing how the world works, knew he would be betrayed, because people (in this case, Judas) often love money and power more than God and his truth. This savvy knowledge and insight helped the man Jesus stay true to his life mission.

True, God tells us we should have a child's heart, but many Christians, said C. S. Lewis, use this as an excuse to justify foolishness. Children often exercise plenty of prudence, and God "wants us to be simple, single-minded, affectionate, and teachable, as good children are." He wants a "grown-up's head" that musters "every bit of intelligence we have to be alert at its job, and in first-class fighting trim. . . . He has room for people with very little sense, but He wants everyone to use what sense they have" (*A Year With C. S. Lewis,* 283).

We are to live with heavenly things in mind *and* with our feet firmly on the ground. We won't be redemptive forces for good if we don't grasp this. Personal piety alone won't cut it, but marry piety to shrewdness, as Jesus did, and you're on your way, Good Guy.

We now have an enhanced and expanded understanding of what masculinity is and isn't. But much of this knowledge will fall flat if we don't roll away another boulder from the front of your CNG tomb. This one's the largest boulder of all, and there's a reason why I held off on it till now— it's a huge portal to a better life and one that we widely avoid, at least at first. It's time to kick one of life's largest imposters offstage. It's time to tell fear to exit stage right.

SEARCHING ONE'S SOUL AND FACING ONE'S FEARS

The wise man in the storm prays to God, not for safety from danger, but for deliverance from fear.
— R A L P H   W A L D O   E M E R S O N

If this God exists and if even you—with your . . . timid lies you used to tell—can change like this, we could all be saints by leaping as you leapt. . . . It's something He can demand of any of us: leap.
— G R A H A M   G R E E N E ,
T H E   E N D   O F   T H E   A F F A I R

If we let things terrify us, life will not be worth living.
— S E N E C A

Christian men in general fear that they won't behave like "Christians should" if they free themselves from expectations I've tried hard to show are biblically unfounded. They fear what their religious leaders will say, what the crowd might think, what their family and friends may do. These are the same exact groups that surrounded Jesus in the Gospels; none always understood or accepted him either, yet he let none stop him. Think about that the next time you ask *WWJD?* Jesus never worshiped at the altar of human approval. But we sure do.

Guys with troubled pasts get to struggle with the false expectations that diminish their lives while also wrestling with these three time zones: their fearful past, their turbulent present, and their anxious future. It's time for them to reset their internal clocks by surrendering to the truth: Life, as it stands, isn't close to the abundance Christ died to give them. Time to get a handle on fear.

SWEET SURRENDER AND REAL HUMILITY

Before I could stare down the fears that haunted me, I had to relinquish my perceived control and admit I needed help. This important step began for me while in a lonely hotel room on a business trip; my wife and family were on the other side of the country. It was in the middle of a cold spell, which was pretty accurate symbolism for my life too. Work wasn't working, and I could tell that all my excuses for myself and blame toward others weren't holding water anymore. I felt somewhat like Job did when he admitted, "I've talked too much, way too much. I'm ready to shut up and listen" (Job 40:5 THE MESSAGE).

Though I couldn't fully see it at the time, a conspiracy of good had me in its grip.

> **A simple equation held my mind captive and would not let me go: *Jesus wasn't always nice. I'm nice. I'm not like Jesus.***

I'd seen the rugged side of Jesus before my trip, and that was changing my view of him, of authentic masculinity. The realization threw me into a period of soul-searching and fear-facing prayer because a simple equation held my mind captive and would not let me go: *Jesus wasn't always nice. I'm nice. I'm not like Jesus.*

And what blew my mind was that though I rarely confessed anything to anyone, admitting this weakness to the Lord felt wonderful! I experienced the benefit James described in his epistle: "God opposes the proud but gives grace to the humble" (4:6).

My surrender experience was aided by life-giving humility, which shouldn't be mistaken for the false humility (the degradation of the true self) that Nice Guys customarily show others so as to hide from criticism and conflict. Being humbled and admitting my needy weakness brought me to the door of one of life's biggest surprises: Our weaknesses can be turned into strengths (Hebrews 11:34). This motivated me to seek wisdom higher than my own, since until then I'd been stuck like a large animal in a mud pit. It made sense that I finally would ask for help; trying to do it on my own had accomplished nothing but sink me deeper.

The fact that humility helped pull me out seemed odd; I'd assumed that humility was pretty much identical to shame. But no, humility brought me clarity and freedom, paving the way to greater knowledge and insight. Humility went before me like John the Baptist, clearing the way for something better to come: the renewing of my mind and the repairing of my heart. Humility got my misconceptions out of the way so God could minister to me with his love.

I was freed from the taskmaster of pretending I had to have all of life's answers. I didn't have to present perfection anymore; I didn't owe the world a 24/7 smile. I was able to say "I don't know" and not feel stressed about it. My craving for control diminished. I didn't have to return every e-mail or phone call ASAP. I could relax for a change. I was comfortable saying nothing or saying "Whatever" to a loaded question or a false accusation.

WHEN "HUMILITY" IS ACTUALLY VIOLENCE TO SELF

It should be clear by now that Nice Guys take powerful and effective spiritual concepts and hide behind them in order to avoid life. This can be particularly well-accomplished with the appearance of humility; humility itself brings life, but when it's twisted into the dark perversion of CNG living, it brings destruction.

Christian Nice Guys turn healthy humility into the distortion of self-effacing self-abuse, usually without others noticing. Secret self-flagellation serves partly to ensure that a CNG's life will never be large or meaningful enough to garner fearsome obstacles or opposition. The apostle Paul specifically warned against the destructive power of faked virtue: "Let no one cheat you of your reward, taking delight in false humility" (Colossians 2:18 NKJV).

God gives each person unique ability or abilities that to some feel like a gift, but to others a curse. Rather than being honest about and embracing what God has freely granted them, CNGs decide to lie about them and say they don't exist. They then compound their dishonesty by hiding their deceit, saying they're "just being a humble Christian."

I know what it's like to hate a gift. In school my IQ put me in the "gifted" category, and I tried to strangle, starve, slap, and shame this uninvited intruder. When it wouldn't die, I pretended it didn't exist.

When it brought attention I did not want, I hollered inside, *People! Just leave me alone!* I wanted to stay below life's radar, but this thing wouldn't let me. It thrust me into the forefront and incited other kids to make fun of me.

I used words they didn't use, more descriptive, more vivid, more colorful than the verbiage common for my age. I was lampooned and mocked. Classmates accused me of showing off when I was being genuine. Trust me—I didn't use words to get attention. I just used words that were bouncing around in my mind.

I dreaded the big clock on the wall hitting the appointed hour, the time when I'd have to leave my usual class and go to the special one. Some of the kids saw this time as a bright shiny rainbow of discovery and adventure; I saw the Grim Reaper double-checking how to spell my last name. Kids glared at me, glared right through me.

Chris, the smelly kid with greasy, long brown hair who sat across from me—he was the worst. He threw sharp pencils at me, one of which stabbed me in the sternum, wagging up and down like a straight animal tail, the type of exaggerated movement you see in cartoons. If it had happened today, my classmates (wide-eyed) would have taken cell phone pictures. It left a tiny circular mark that lasted for many years.

My teacher usually eyed me with a disappointed bewilderment, like he was examining his tax bill. Fully aware of my shoddy grades, his look when I'd leave for this class said, *If this kid's gifted, I'm Captain Kangaroo.* My mother, upon hearing that I was beneficially different, said, "Him?! He can't even find his shoes in the morning!" Something that should have been nurtured at home and at school was instead undercut, which, not coincidentally, is another goal of false humility.

I pretended my ability didn't exist. I buried it (or tried to) under the ash heap of faked virtue, a positive I perverted into a negative. This unholy and unauthorized burial, the poorest of stewardship, would haunt me for decades.

FEAR FACTORS: EVERY NICE GUY'S ENEMY

The next step toward every CNG's abundant life is mind renewal and heart unbinding, which requires an understanding of fear's role. "If I were to identify one common factor at the core of every problem experienced by Nice Guys," says Dr. Robert Glover in *No More Mr. Nice Guy*, "it would be *fear*." Nice guys process voluminous information through "fear-encrusted neurons in their brains," a difficult cycle to break. Paradoxically, they have both fear of failure and fear of success, just as I did.

I mentioned earlier that when I realized my dire predicament, I sought higher wisdom. I took inventory of life indicators that showed I wasn't really living, and I shared them with someone who better knew what fear does to a man. Decades-old roadblocks were then removed, and off I went toward a vitalized, abundant life.

> **Paradoxically, Nice Guys have both fear of failure and fear of success.**

God's Word aided the renewing of my mind. I was able to embrace what he really thinks about me—and, therefore, what is actually true about me—as well as genuinely hear his warnings against living naïvely. Here are some key verses that helped break fear's once jailer-like control of me:

(1) "I alone know my purpose for you, says the Lord: prosperity and

not misfortune, and a long line of children after you. If you invoke me and pray to me, I will listen to you" (Jeremiah 29:11–12 NEB). It's vital that Nice Guys realize this; many believe that God (and life in general) is out to get them. They don't believe their futures are bright, and they'll have even more difficulty grasping this promise if they attend a church that over-dwells on sin and shame at the expense of grace and freedom.

(2) Jesus' warning in John 16:33 helped take away my shock-response (of numbness and passivity) to injustice: "In this world you *will* have trouble. But take heart! I have overcome the world" (emphasis added). CNGs should memorize and focus on this truth until their philosophy ("If I live small, my troubles will be few") no longer makes sense to them. If earthly trouble is inevitable, living small is not the answer; that just means the Nice Guy pointlessly lives small and has troubles all the same.

(3) An evil will wants to destroy our lives, and few things destroy more effectively than fear. Satan is the father of lies (John 8:44), so CNGs need to view their fear issue as a spiritual battle, one that includes fighting against the internal belief that we are worthless and will never amount to much, lies many of us were told (in various ways) as young boys. They partially wage this battle by obeying Jesus' words to pray for deliverance from the evil one (Matthew 6:13).

(4) "You did not receive a spirit that makes you a slave again to fear, but you received the Spirit of sonship. And by him we cry, 'Abba, Father' " (Romans 8:15). Meditate on this, along with "God did not give us a spirit of timidity, but a spirit of power, of love and of self-discipline" (2 Timothy 1:7); you'll see that God actively opposes fear—it's not part of the life he wants for you.

(5) Consider these words from Revelation 21: "The cowardly . . . their place will be in the fiery lake of burning sulfur. This is the second death" (v. 8). I don't understand everything in Revelation, but I can tell from this passage that being cowardly does not please God. As mentioned earlier, Protestants are quick to point out the sins of commission (active participa-tion) compared with those of omission—sins that occur when we *don't* do

something, which Catholics emphasize. *God is not fooled by our passive cowardice.*

OPTIMISM, YOUR ESTRANGED HELPER

A new perspective enlivened my days when fear was cast down. *Optimism* had been an estranged character; now he began to stir up the dirt in my life, cleaning house, kicking out freeloading (often cynical) thoughts that burdened me. Believing in God's goodness changed how I viewed my future, helping to regulate my thought patterns and sharpening my mental abilities. There's growing evidence that this very change in thinking is one of the best ways to ward off depression and related maladies like listlessness, which leads to directionless living.

Optimism is an antidote to one of the seven deadly sins, or what were originally referred to as the "eight bad thoughts." There used to be eight, anyway, until some Christian monks, seventeen centuries ago, rolled the sin of *acedia* into the sin of sloth, which isn't accurate. *Acedia,* from a Greek word meaning "without care," denotes indifference to one's life and to the surrounding world. Sloth describes a general laziness and a specific aversion to work; CNGs aren't lazy but they *are* primarily indifferent. This is where deep-seated fear and passionless living lead: a lukewarm existence that pretends it's somehow virtuous to sit on the sidelines.

Optimism fueled greater critical thinking in me. Using my thoughts for good helped to combat a defining smallness of mind and lack of common sense; shrewdness finally reported for duty. Optimism facilitates willingness to take risks and to live with the consequences—it breeds courage and a choice to embrace even failure for the purpose of learning and growth.

Optimism is also beneficial for health. Harvard graduates who were most pessimistic in 1946 were also the least healthy when restudied in 1980. Virginia Tech students who were pessimistic suffered more colds, sore throats, and flus. Optimistic people likewise recover better from cancer and surgery.

Keep in mind, though, that, as with all good things, you can overdo it:

Unchecked optimism, much like hyper-spiritualism, can spell endless frustration and even traumatic disaster if you aren't informed and savvy. In order to be wise as a serpent, follow this recipe: Mix in all the optimism that comes your way (optimism brings newfound hope); then add some shrewdness (like that seen in the life of Jesus) to help you figure out which events in your life you can regulate or control and which you cannot.

MIND YOUR BUSINESS

> **Unchecked optimism, much like hyper-spiritualism, can spell endless frustration and even traumatic disaster if you aren't informed and savvy.**

Another effective way to reduce or eliminate the many slippery detours of fear is urging yourself to *mind your business*. Even though on the surface they appear slow to accept help or generosity, Nice Guys (often through passive-aggression) actually look to others to take care of them in most every area of life. CNGs frequently expect others to chart their future.

Our parents were the only ones required to take care of us. Some did, some didn't. If they failed, it's up to *you*—not your wife, girlfriend, boss, minister, children, whoever—to do something about it. Remember: You've got one *Daddy*, and as you get a handle on fear you'll increasingly see and know that he's all for you, looking out for you. *No one on this earth is accountable to bring you what you need or want.* It's not up to your wife or girlfriend to fill your emotional holes. That work is yours. Your boss isn't on the hook to provide a living for you. That's your job. It's not your minister's role to maintain your relationship with God. That's up to you. Your kids are yours to nurture, not yours to nurture you. *This is how real men live—not in a codependent vacuum, but in a vital state of healthy connection and interaction with others.*

When fear takes a hike, so will your belief that you have no choices. Your vistas will expand. Your options will increase. You'll finally see that you have a say in the quality of your life—and, gloriously, that God's grace ˙bsolutely real. You'll take care of your own life. You'll stop being a moral meter maid for others, wasting time and energy subtly pressuring them to "behave." You'll now have this time and energy to bring your own heart and mind before God and examine them.

In harmony with God's will, you'll make progress in the direction he wants you to go and become more proactive in your responsibilities. You'll see yourself and others accurately. You'll accept that no one else can be your ultimate advocate. You are your own manager, pilot, press secretary, attorney—you get the picture.

Courage will finally flow. It will grow weak at times, but that's life— don't mistake courage's natural waning as its exit. Remember, there aren't two types of people: those who never grow weak and those who do. Courageous people aren't always so; they're flawed humans like everyone else, yet they manage to push through the low times, partly because they don't waste precious energy on self-beatings.

When fear is dealt a substantial blow and you start minding your own business, you will become far more protective about your life than before. You will fight for a better existence, not because you're selfish, but because you want to be a wise steward of this gift from God.

You won't feel the need to apologize for this new attitude either. You won't allow unnecessary abuse and suffering, not because you have something to prove (other people's opinions will matter less) but because you have something profound to protect. You will choose to lay down your rights when it's befitting and virtuous. When you withdraw from a situation, you'll do so in an *active* manner because fear will no longer govern you.

I can tell when I stop minding my own business. I think more than I should about what others think about me. I lose momentum and courage, and I get sidetracked about the petty issues. I call this sliding down Mount Assertive; nevertheless, I never slip completely off and tumble back to the Valley of Passivity. (Remember: passivity is now a temptation, not a lifestyle.)

Even if I fall back from time to time to a base camp here or there, it's not the end of the world. Expect it. It doesn't mean the death of your personal growth. Relax. When this happens, admit it without beating yourself up and becoming a drama king. Remember, you're human, and being human is not a sin.

The best way to get back up to that summit is to get our focus on our life mission.

LIFE MISSION

Part of your path out of the CNG life and into true masculinity is the embracing of a *life mission*. While this term and concept initially sound threatening or overwhelming to many, forming a personal mission is not as difficult as it might seem. Try taking the following non-intimidating steps.

(1) *Work with your passion.* This is more than simply looking for something comfortable and convenient, like a hobby. It's asking yourself, *What did I dream about before I stopped dreaming?* Your passion is usually what you're good at or want to be good at; during the inevitable dry times and difficult seasons, you'll need this passion to complete the work required of you and to persevere in your responsibilities. If you're doing what you love, even the hardest situations can be tempered by the fact that you've found your fit.

> **Working with your passion is asking yourself, *What did I dream about before I stopped dreaming?***

(2) *Work with the pain in your (gulp) heart.* This is where "blessed dissatisfaction" comes into play. No one likes pain, but eventually former CNGs say they came to view pain as an expert teacher. Haddon Robinson, professor of preaching at Gordon-Conwell Theological Seminary, says change often happens like this: Pain + time + insight = change. Nice Guys already have plenty of pain, and they have time too; they presently lack the insight needed to move away from their swamp of stuckness. If handled properly, Nice Guy pain can bless others with wise counsel and spiritual healing; learn to ask yourself, *Is there an aspect of suffering that calls for my attention?* If so, then take your ~t in the action!

Asking myself this question has resulted in this book and other related endeavors. We males are so accustomed to ignoring our hearts that we forget—or maybe we don't even know—that the passion, insight, and instinct from our hearts are needed; *we* are needed. The enemy knows this, and he wants to steal your heart, rendering you ineffective. Your pain can be a redemptive force for good if you allow yourself to experience it and learn from it while relying on the help of the Holy Spirit. Our hearts are an absolutely vital source of masculine power and discernment, as Jesus showed when grieving over Lazarus (John 11:35).

(3) *Work with what's at hand.* Nice Guys often live in the future, suspending their opportunities to have a fulfilling life in the present. After being unrealistic about how life plays out, they then complain about life passing them by; while they frequently believe they have some kind of grand summit they must reach first, the world really needs their passion, energy, and resources *now.* Most people's lives will contain no single act of greatness; even so, they can take part in acts of kindness with heart-driven passion and genuine love. *Spiritual maturity is found where Christ said it is, in loving God and your neighbor.*

> **Most people's lives will contain no single act of greatness; even so, they can take part in acts of kindness with heart-driven passion and genuine love. Spiritual maturity is found where Christ said it is, in loving God and your neighbor.**

EXPECT TO FALTER

When I made substantial life changes, people noticed and applauded, which initially felt great. But then I started thinking like Jerry Maguire did while undergoing his big change. Tom Cruise plays the sports agent who has a sudden moment of conviction and decides he must get honest; he stays up all night writing a heartfelt, compelling manifesto that proposes sweeping changes within his agency and his industry. He's never felt more alive than while writing that document, which he photocopies and le⁀ in the mail slots for all his colleagues the next morning. His heart is s⁀

with meaning and purpose. He's flooded with relief to be a source of redemption in that screwed-up domain.

His soul is glad—for about a half hour. Then comes the onslaught of fear like a pounding parade. He can't beat it back, he loses his nerve and his courage, and he tries to retrieve his manifesto before anyone can read it. Too late: He has unleashed (and cannot stop) a chain of momentous events. He suddenly wants his life to go back to "normal," even though normal was killing him.

I don't know how many times I awoke around two in the morning, stared out the front window, and proceeded to berate myself. *What have I done? People just don't do what you did, Paul—leave their job to pursue a dream? You have three kids, man. What about your family?* I was tempted to give it all up and dive back toward the perception of safety.

I used to read the Old Testament antics of the Israelites and shake my head, thinking I'd have handled things so much better. Freed from Egyptian captivity, and now some actually want to go back into bondage? *This can't be accurate,* I said to myself when I was younger and knew everything. *People would never willingly go back to slavery.*

Actually, they would, and they do. I almost did it myself. I'm either guilty or capable of every Israelite sin. I *am* every Israelite. I even fantasized about going back to my old dungeon. In my weak moments of fearfulness, security and familiarity felt better than freedom and purpose, which carry the risk of the unknown; this will likely be true for you also at one point or another. George Bernard Shaw said, "The slave of fear: the worst of slaveries."

FEED FACTS TO FEAR

Former Christian Nice Guys tell me they went through similar pivotal-moment battles in their minds and hearts. Treat these times like a scientist treats a beloved experiment going in a different direction than he anticipated: *Stick to the facts, and feed them to fear.* Says Marilyn Ferguson:

Fear is a question: what are you afraid of, and why? Just as the seed of health is in illness, because illness contains information, your fears are a treasure-house of self-knowledge if you explore them.

Well, what about my family? I mused. I *had* prepared financially for this moment, retooling our finances to where we could live off less. Having worked at a chamber of commerce, I knew that most new career ventures go under for lack of capital, so we'd consistently squirreled away money. I'd also figured out how to make some non-labor-based income for backup—we were ready, and my family wouldn't go without.

What about changing careers? I continued. I had tolerated workplace guff that would curl your hair if you heard it; I did so for years. Now I was fighting back with action, turning my dissatisfaction into motivation toward a better life for me and my family.

And so what *if I make a mistake?* People make mistakes, right? I mean, I'd made plenty of them already, following the timid path. Life goes on. Again, why should it be more terrifying to risk mistakes by being proactive?

How I wish I could guarantee you won't fear again; my, the books that sell just by telling people what they want to hear. But you don't need any more sweet-smelling smoke blown in your face—you need the facts. My better life didn't come without some fear, and, chances are, neither will yours. Fear doesn't go away when you try to leave Niceland, but, when

> **You won't eliminate fear during this lifetime, but you will learn to use fear as a motivator; you won't be fearless, but you will fear *less*.**

properly confronted, it no longer stops you either. Putting the facts to fear moves it toward manageability and gradually reduces it before your eyes; ultimately, you'll be better able to see whether you're experiencing something that does need to be considered or are instead simply being emotionally assaulted by your enemies.

You won't eliminate fear during this lifetime, but instead of being captive to fear you can move through it. You will learn to use fea motivator; you won't be fearless, but you will fear *less*. Fear will become a cue to proactivity just as hunger is a cue to eat.

RENEWING YOUR MIND THROUGH LOVING FELLOWSHIP

We noted Robert Glover's observation that Nice Guys process a lot of information through "fear-encrusted neurons in their brains." There's mounting evidence showing how children who are not emotionally nurtured may literally be unable to empathize with others because the portion of the brain that stimulates such feelings didn't properly develop. Childhood abuse, for example, may literally change a person's brain.

Even so, God is merciful. He has provided a way toward rejuvenation, a metamorphosis that develops through love. Science has also demonstrated that the exchange of genuine love—part of what the Bible refers to as fellowship—may neurologically impact the brain, which, for instance, can help the CNG to literally overcome fear. We are to be transformed through the renewing of our mind (Romans 12:2); you'll be amazed by the strength and boldness building inside you as you become convinced that you are loved by other human beings.

What's wrong with men being more truthful, honest, protective, authentic, loving, genuine, passionate, thirsty for life guided by the Holy Spirit?

When fear and anxiety are dealt serious blows, the power that's released is remarkable, akin to a new life, a kind of baptism. For this to occur, we'll have to overcome something more dreaded than the IRS, public speaking, tarantulas, and the abominations people drink and eat on *Fear Factor:* We'll have to embrace change. Most people hate change, which is why most Christian Nice Guys also hate their lives.

friends of CNGs are often troubled when seeing large-
their men, worrying that they won't know (or perhaps
d version. For these concerned (and yet nearsighted) souls,
ion: What's wrong with men being more truthful, honest,

protective, authentic, loving, genuine, passionate, thirsty for life guided by the Holy Spirit? When fear is given the boot, we're talking about the creation of masculine men, not macho morons.

While relational support can be a tremendous boost to the journey out from passivity, I've nonetheless noticed a disturbing truth regarding this fundamental CNG issue: Some don't really want to get better. They're content with their smaller lives and their timid lies that actualize hell on earth, a reluctance that brings clarity to a Jesus-question that used to puzzle me. "Do you want to get well?" he asked the ill man at the pool of Bethesda (John 5:6). Did he ask because he knew that some people don't want to be well? I don't know for sure, but I think so. I know he was shrewd enough to see through false statements and motives, bold and righteous enough to point them out.

You've picked up this book, you've read nearly the entire thing, and now you must ask yourself the same foundational question: *Do I want to get well?* You've invested this time on your Nice Guy dilemma, facing the mirror of your life. After all this distance, one more step is now required: Do you want to get rid of the fear and anxiety that diminish you? They won't go away on their own. They must be confronted, ideally with the help of someone who's gone before and walked with others who are making the journey.

I would have chosen sin by not confronting my fear, and I suspect that would also be the case for you—remember, *missing the mark* is one of the root concepts behind our sin. God wants us to stop sinning because sin is bad for us and others and because he's on our side—he wants us ever closer to the plentiful life for which he created us.

Right now you're not as useful as you could be; fear and anxiety are standing in the way. Confront them, and you'll start a chain reaction: They will flee, and their accomplices will begin to slink away. When someone I love realized it was time for her to go into an addiction program, she said that my words of how fear is an imposter that will back down kept her from running back to her car as she continued through the clinic's doors; she also saw me face my fear and win. Brothers, you can either stay in your current mire and become yet another casualty of a life misspent, or you can rise up, face change, and leap into a life that glorifies God. Is there really a choice?

Having heard this before doesn't make it less true: The first step is the hardest *and* the most rewarding. This is where Christian men should be of good cheer, for in this sense we have it easier than other men. When we believed and were saved, we renounced an old way of life and faced the fear of something new. It's now time to take a similar step: You showed courage following Jesus—now show courage facing fear.

NO MORE MR. NICE GUY: PRACTICAL HELP FOR YOUR NEW LIFE AHEAD

Pray not for lighter burdens, but for stronger backs.

— TEDDY ROOSEVELT

"[King] David and his men are fierce."

— 2 SAMUEL 17:8

There's a better life for Christian men (and their loved ones) who recognize that false expectations have been placed upon them and who finally see how seemingly constructive niceness is often destructive passivity in disguise. CNGs who successfully battle the fear that once owned them will uncover and possess even greater knowledge, and their transformation into a Christian Good Guy will be even more dramatic.

The following is some practical advice that will assist you in being wise as a serpent as you walk in this new way, a way that doesn't bully or beg. There are a few key facts that can help you discover and maintain this Christlike life—the assertive life.

MAKE YOUR NEEDS (DEMANDS) AND WANTS (REQUESTS) CLEAR

Atop the list of insights: It is *not* sinful to have normal (God-given) wants and needs. They don't make you "worldly" either—they make you human. All relationships, outside of slavery, include interactive give-and-take. Contrary to what you've been told by some Scripture twisters, you are not a slave—in bondage—to other people. Rather, *you are an agent of God's redemptive power* (as opposed to a selfish force) *that serves other people as you choose.* Sometimes, for instance, this means telling people no without giving a long explanation or having a concrete reason that they need to hear.

Think of your life as your garden. You don't let just anything into the soil, and you don't let anyone come in and dig a bunch of holes. You even pull out unwanted plants so that more beneficial plants can grow. A healthy garden has a discerning gardener. A healthy life is a selective life.

Demanding people drive most of us crazy, and after one of them has scorched part of our life, we often sit back and think, *Man, all he had to do was ask—I would have done it.* Inversely, also keep this in mind when you demand something of another person; though we should require respect and truthfulness from others, we need not necessarily behave in a demanding way. Oftentimes, a sincere and clear request will get the job done. Don't use a hammer when pliers work better. Anne Lamott puts it this way: "You don't always have to chop with the sword of truth. You can point with it too" (*Bird by Bird*).

I suggest starting with smaller straightforward requests, then gradually moving forward. For example, you may not want to come out of your new-life gate by demanding a fat raise; you'd likely see better results by first working on your negotiation skills. (By the way, here's a negotiating tip: If possible, let the other person speak first, then seek to be the one who asks the questions. When it comes to money, someone's going to have the upper hand in the conversation; why not you?)

Use "I want/need" statements combined with what you want or need, and don't apologize for asking; Jesus tells us to be honest about what we believe and desire: "Simply let your 'Yes' be 'Yes,' and your 'No,' 'No'; anything beyond this comes from the evil one" (Matthew 5:37). This evil one is the enemy Christian Nice Guys battle all the time, and because they so frequently are dishonest with what they think and feel, they often lie through both commission (overt, explicit) and omission (subtle or unspoken).

As with deception, it's similarly important that you do not approach your needs and wants from a position of anger. (When you internalize unfettered anger, you often leave opportunities for other people to have partial ownership of your mind.) CNGs have a lot of pent-up frustration, and when they finally realize how badly others have treated them—see the injustice done to them—they want to *unload*. However, what they need to acknowledge is that they have allowed the injustice. No one put a gun to their head. They alone allowed its entrance into their lives, so even though they're not responsible for the choices that others have made, they still suffer the consequences of their own actions and inactions. Try this: Take your mind off your offender and put your focus onto the kind of barrier or boundary you need to build in order not to be susceptible again.

Consider writing a personal Declaration of Independence from the error of living to please others ("the disease to please"); doing so can help to bring you into embracing normal wants and needs. It's okay to have an opinion, to be angry and not sin, to embrace your healthy sexual desires, to be respected at work and to find another job if you aren't. *You have intrinsic rights.* Ruth Koch and Kenneth Haugk have presented the matter in this way:

> We are created in God's image—so Genesis 1:27 tells us, and we believe it. We are loved by God—so John 3:16 tells us, and we believe it. There are no distinctions to be made among us—so Galatians 3:28 tells us, and we believe it. We are priests, all of us, a royal priesthood—so 1 Peter 2:9 tells us, and we believe it. These are the good earth from which our basic human rights spring. (*Speaking the Truth in Love*)

From this they conclude that all people have the right to be treated with respect; to say no without explanation and without guilt; to slow down and take time to think; to change their mind; to ask for what they want; to ask for information and help; to make mistakes; to make choices and accept the consequences of those choices; to own and express feelings; to maintain a separate self that is accountable to God and independent of the expectations, approval, or influence of others.

By the way, part of making your requests clear is not talking on and on. The usual guideline: Less is better. Jack Welch, former CEO of General Electric, says, "Every idea you present must be something you could get across easily at a cocktail party with strangers." Sometimes I broadly write down my insights and then pare the words from that point before sharing them with others. Anyway, short and crisp is good for you and it's respectful to the person you're communicating with.

BETTER SEX

> **Do not blame your wife for the poor quality of your intimacy. Nice Guys make their own sorrowful bed; they settle for less, and you often get what you settle for.**

For a number of reasons, the CNG often settles for low-quality intimacy with his wife. Not all of these factors are within his control, but before he addresses his cancerous fear, he usually doesn't show much masculine energy, making him less desirable. Once fear gets mashed, his sexual drive and his attractiveness grow; in a culture that mishandles a man's passions and desires, his wife might not yet understand the power of his God-given wants and needs. It's up to *you*, Christian Good Guy, to explain it to her. Consider reading to her what I wrote in chapter 6 ("We're Men, Not Eunuchs"); that section's humor is intentional, designed to lighten this serious topic and make it easier for people to hear and receive truths about these relational realities.

Next, do not blame your wife for the poor quality of your intimacy.

Not only would this make matters worse, chances are it's inaccurate. Again, Nice Guys make their own sorrowful bed; they settle for less, and you often get what you settle for. Refusal to be direct with sexual desires puts wives on eggshells, making sex an anxious rather than an exciting topic.

One of the wisest pieces of advice I received regarding sexual intimacy came from Kevin Leman, who famously pointed out that "sex begins in the kitchen"—that is, sex begins in the mind and works its way forward from there. Anticipation is a great thing, especially when you have little ones around. Busy lives demand scheduling, and though this probably doesn't sound very romantic, you will likely need to schedule intimacy—not on some secret calendar but, rather, being realistic and paving the way by being forthright about your hopes and needs. Being direct about sex opens the door to enhanced intimacy.

Disillusioned Christian Nice Guys haven't relinquished their desire for control in the making of intimacy—this is a romance killer. Happy Christian Good Guys let sexual activity unfold, because sexual pleasure is the unfolding and releasing of sexual energy. The pleasure is in *both* the journey and the destination.

One suggestion: If your current method of communication involves showering your wife with attention, and that isn't working, consider pulling back to some degree. Sometimes the best way to pull your spouse toward you is to create some distance—even if it sounds counterproductive, try being a little aloof. Instead of touching her all the time, be selective; don't be cold, but don't smother her either. Former CNGs say this approach has helped create the kind of intimacy they'd always wanted.

BE CAREFUL WITH CHRISTIAN TESTIMONIES

Church testimonies, from either laymen or leaders, can be tricky business for CNGs. In order to accelerate your progress down the Christian Good Guy highway, heed Pastor Steve Brown's warning to exercise critical thinking:

> Time after time I have heard brothers and sisters tell how God had changed them, healed them, and sanctified them. I used to have a suspicion that they were lying. Since becoming a pastor I am no longer suspicious—I know. A lot of the testimony we hear in the church is either a lie or has covered the truth so well that it is the same thing as a lie. (Steve Brown, in Dr. Robert Grover, *No More Mr. Nice Guy,* 176).

Brown doesn't say all testimony is deceitful, but he's being wise when he says that some (a lot) is. He's alerting us for a good reason: False testimony is one of the strongest taskmasters in your spiritual life, holding you to yet another set of unmeetable expectations.

I once attended a church where the pastor often held himself up as the hero of his own stories, a consistent example of virtuous and victorious Christian living. This was an impossible level of achievement, at least for me and many others, but we had only a few weekly hours to observe his life—we weren't privy to anything outside of church services.

He would testify to amazing victories over sin and how such sin would completely leave him once "ultimate victory" was achieved. That had no parallel with my life. All sorts of sin just seemed to make camp around me; of course I'd fight off temptation, but it was as likely to be back the next day as the mailman. This pastor's "testimonies" left me feeling hopeless.

Once I was experiencing this spiritual malaise while in my car, waiting to turn left at a red light. I wasn't quick to respond when it changed—I was somewhat wrapped up in my thoughts—so when I looked up and noticed the green, I instinctively checked my rearview mirror to see if I had impeded anyone else. There was my pastor, right behind me, beating the snot out of his steering wheel, his face contorted in rage. I couldn't hear what he was yelling, but it sure wasn't a blessing.

Another person's anguish over being slightly delayed had never been so liberating! *This guy behaves as childishly and foolishly as I do, and he's older than me too!* I thought. He presented himself from the pulpit as sterling silver, yet there on the common blacktop of life he was human just like the rest of us. For me, a naïve perception started falling to the floorboards, and I was instantly more comfortable in my own skin, set free by a tizzy fit.

The tyranny of dishonest Christian testimony is that it diminishes true boldness. You compare yourself to a standard that doesn't exist; you find yourself lacking, and you disqualify yourself from the game of life because you believe you don't have what's necessary and required. On some level you begin to think there are two kinds of men; those who constantly (or even unfailingly) achieve all kinds of victory, and those (like you) who don't. In legalistic churches, sometimes almost everyone's trapped—the leaders play incredible games to keep sin hidden so they don't get the boot, and the flock loses heart from trying to live by their unlivable standards. *This is not authentic, it's not Christian, and it's not living!*

I compare those years of being pastored by the self-proclaimed hero to the years I spent with Tom Sabens, pastor of Table Rock Fellowship in Central Point, Oregon. I don't think Tom knows how liberating his honesty was to me, how it set me free, helped me to live larger. He's usually the *goat* of his own stories, and he

> **The tyranny of dishonest Christian testimony is that it diminishes true boldness.**

has shared more heart-wrenching accounts of his failures than any other man I know. My favorite was about a morning fight with his dear wife, Jane. Tom had to leave (or flee) for work, and as he was driving away in his VW Bug, in the rearview mirror he saw Jane running after him; Tom was reminded about the state of their marriage as leftover toast slapped his window.

Tom is a secure man who doesn't believe he has to be nice all the time, so he can afford to be weak in front of others. I've seen him take surprising risks by letting people into ministry who wouldn't have a chance at most other churches. These gifted, troubled souls had great screw-up potential—their reputations preceded them—but still, Tom took the chance. He's comfortable with risk because he knows he serves a good (not a nice) God. Because fear doesn't own Tom, he's free to be good instead of nice, and in this way he frees others from the tyranny of taskmasters like false Christian testimonies.

LEARN HOW TO SPOT LYING

We're told never to lie, but we're almost never instructed on how to discern dishonesty. Emphasis on personal piety with ignorance of wise living doesn't make sense; doesn't integrity include insight and perception? Jesus said to be innocent as doves *and* wise as serpents. Nice Guys are often the last to know, and there's nothing Christlike about being ignorant.

Most people aren't good at lying, and their behavior gives them away because deception makes them nervous. If the person you're talking with does one or two of the following, he or she may just be nervous; if he does more, you're likely on to something false. Put on your Good Guy glasses and take a closer look.

EYE-CONTACT CHANGES

People usually make eye contact one-quarter to one-half of the time. If suddenly, at what might be a convenient moment to lie, the person speaking to you is glancing around or looking away, beware; he might be keeping track of who else around could contradict his words. (Experienced liars may look for a distraction that will rapidly change the subject.) Sometimes you'll be able to see the white on the top and bottom of his eyes rather than just the sides.

VOICE AND WORDS CHANGE

Note any increase in the use of *ums, ahs,* or *ers.* Sometimes a liar's pitch goes up or down, or the rate of speech becomes faster or slower than usual. Liars often fire off serial excuses, each one more questionable than the last; sometimes the excuses even contradict each other, when the liar doesn't have time to think about whether or not his story works.

One study suggests that liars are less likely to use first-person words such as *I* or *my* in speech and writing; they also may exclude emotional words like *hurt* or *angry* in favor of cognitive words like *comprehend* and *realize*.

BODY LANGUAGE CHANGES

A liar may sweat or blush, two difficult-to-hide reactions. He may turn his body away from you, even slightly. His legs may start jiggling. He may constantly adjust his hair or suddenly scratch. He may cover a part of his face, especially his mouth.

GUT INSTINCTS

Experienced liars are skilled at controlling their eyes, voice, words, and body language. Accordingly, you need to listen to your gut: Don't ignore it. In addition, reserve judgment for another time, when (and if) you have more information. Don't accuse too quickly, and if your instinct turns out to be correct, you'll be glad you didn't immediately confront a practiced liar—if he's good at lying, chances are he's good at exonerating himself when accused. It's one thing to *accuse* and entirely another to *prove*.

CAUTION: SOME WILL BE ENRAGED BY YOUR STRENGTH

Mark 5 records an amazing illustration of how sin distorts. Jesus healed a tortured man, possessed by demons that even chains could not restrain. How did the people of the area respond to this miracle—with celebration? By bowing in worship? Did they ask for healing also? No. "They began to beg Jesus to depart from their region." *They begged a healer to go away.* I used to think no one would really give that response if they were faced with that opportunity. Then I was healed and saw for myself.

Christian Nice Guys who become Christian Good Guys will find that some around them were very happy with them just as they were. They will criticize the Christian Good Guy and want the Christian Nice Guy back. They might be agitated, furious with, and even fearful of your newfound masculinity.

Most of the reasons for this revolve around power: The weak becoming strong disrupts the order of things, and people don't like their worlds to change much, especially when they lose a perceived advantage. The people who felt powerful when you were nice and weak are usually unhealthy people who probably still have some influence in your life, unless you decide otherwise.

Nice Guy: It's not your role to rehabilitate the troubled people who like you flabby and pliable. Instead of trying to fix them, tell them what you think and how you feel and then move on. Your thoughts and feelings should be valued; don't justify them to people who think you shouldn't have thoughts and feelings. Those who have control in your life want you to possess *their* thoughts and feelings—they don't want you to be you, and, as hopefully you know by now, God wants you to be you. Being you is the only way you're going to live out your purpose and find fulfillment during this life.

> **Requiring respect doesn't mean you'll get it; disrespectful people just want you to make them feel powerful again. They're after a rush, and you're their drug of choice. Take yourself off the market.**

If you let them, controlling people will spend hours trying to get you to justify yourself; they'll pick you apart and demand complete access to your inner world. Jesus didn't allow just anyone into his interior world—keeping a part of yourself separate is not a sin. Put an end to accusing questions with something like "Because I said so" or "That's the way I am." Show that you mean business, that you value your heart and mind and that others should too. If someone doesn't, why let him influence your life?

In some ways, such a person (a nemesis, because, in a way, he can't be overcome) is worse than an enemy. Most enemies don't like you *because* of what you think and feel and say. A nemesis has the same disregard, but additionally endeavors to overthrow your inner life; in this sense, enemies are more respectful.

Don't spend hours trying to change a nemesis; those conversations are like beating heads against a wall, getting both of you nowhere and leaving you in substantial pain. Requiring respect doesn't mean you'll get it; disrespectful people just want you to make them feel powerful again. They're after a rush, and you're their drug of choice. Take yourself off the market.

That you will earn a few enemies should bring some solace. You earned some enemies playing the Nice Guy game, so at least now you're upsetting others for the right reasons. As Mark Twain mused, Jesus said to pray for your enemies; he never said you couldn't have any.

People will lie about you and gossip when they can, and how you respond will determine part of your journey out of the CNG ghetto. Confront such damage wherever it's to your advantage, which may mean not confronting it at all. You can't block all of the unfair arrows fired at you, and it's a waste of your time to try. Remember, minding your own business does not mean correcting or pleasing everyone in your life. Stay true to your mission, and remember these words by James Thurber: "Do not look back in anger, or forward in fear, but around in awareness."

OUR CHILDREN: SERVED UP SOFT

I would be remiss if I didn't address the epidemic of raising children to be Christian Nice Guys and Gals, because we're rearing another generation to follow in our bland mediocrity. I've been warning about this for more than a decade on Christian radio: It's so much easier to raise healthy boys and girls than to repair shattered ones.

A compelling article in *Psychology Today* says we are "A Nation of Wimps" whose parents are going to "ludicrous lengths to take the lumps and bumps out of life for their children." It's sad that it would take a secular warning to awaken the church; however, this is something that God does when his people refuse to listen to wisdom. The following words are considered almost blasphemous today, especially in the overprotective church: "Kids need to feel badly sometimes," says child psychologist David Elkind.

> With few challenges of their own, kids are unable to forge their creative adaptations to the normal vicissitudes of life. That not only makes them risk-averse, it makes them psychologically fragile, riddled with anxiety. In the process they're robbed of identity, meaning and a sense of accomplishment, to say nothing of a shot at real happiness. Forget, too, about perseverance, not simply a moral virtue but a necessary life skill. These turn out to be the spreading psychic fault lines of 21st-century youth. Whether we want to or not, we're on our way to creating a nation of wimps. ("A Nation of Wimps," *Psychology Today* [Nov./Dec. 2004])

I'm concerned that this rampant societal problem is even worse within the church. Having fielded countless phone calls from Christian parents, I believe that in our well-intentioned attempts to protect our children from sin, we're keeping them from life. We too often blur the line between vigilance and paranoia. I've seen what "sweet Christian girls" do in college after escaping their overprotective homes; their parents would tear their clothing and sit in ashes if they only knew. "These kids have been controlled for so long, they just go crazy," admits John Portmann, professor of religious studies at the University of Virginia.

Many young people are becoming Nice Guys and Gals right before our eyes—more responsive to the herd, too eager to fit in, less assertive in the classroom, unwilling to disagree with peers, afraid to question authority. All this is antithetical to real life in Christ; in fact, it's a spirit of antichrist.

The sons and daughters of Christian Nice Guys have seen many more examples of living out the gentle virtues than the rugged ones. We have them isolated, immobile, and we're telling them to respect a subculture that in many ways doesn't deserve their respect. We're more concerned about providing them with coddled safety than we are about inspiring them to live as God desires. *We're raising spiritual veal.*

Rabbi Shmuley Boteach argues, "Your job as a parent is to ease that transition between the idyllic world of the sandbox and the cold world of adulthood as much as humanly possible." This transition is *not* achieved through sequestered seclusion. Our kids need to see us venturing boldly into the tough side of life and handling conflict with wisdom and courage.

I once ended a business deal with someone who was being increasingly abusive. His false accusations weren't the end of the world, but they bugged me, and I knew other ones were coming from him as well. The knowledge of additional (still coming) allegations put me on eggshells—I wasted energy by working up in my mind what I would say, and I wasted time counterpunching criticisms (present and future) that weren't even accurate.

He was a busy guy who rarely took my phone calls; I usually couldn't talk with him directly, so this time I wrote him a letter. I didn't go on and on defending myself, but instead constructed a short and pithy paragraph explaining that I didn't like the relationship and was ending the deal. I didn't call him names, and I didn't beg him to change. I wished him well with his future endeavors.

When I showed the letter to my sons and daughter, Garrett came alive. "I love that you wrote that, Dad!" he yelled with so much energy I could have put cables on his earlobes and jumpstarted a motor home. He was proud of his old man, and how could I not feel better as well? Anyway, wouldn't you know it, my business partner contacted me right away. We worked it out. It didn't end our relationship. Assertiveness and proactivity fortified it.

As mentioned earlier, my daughter, Abby, has my go-ahead to embrace the rugged virtues, which includes defending herself physically and emotionally. She's free and comfortable with her own power to act, and because of this, she's willing to sacrifice herself for others. (*That's* virtue.)

Just before I was to speak to Abby's first-grade class on writing, her teacher, Mrs. McCoy, asked the kids what they thought about Abby. One girl, the only student with a missing limb, spoke of admiration.

"She saved me. I think Abby—" she gave an adorable dramatic pause—
"is a good person."

I later found out that Abby had fought for and rescued her one-armed classmate from two girls determined to beat her up. (Aren't boys supposed to be the physical bullies?) Abby got scratched on her face while defending a physically challenged person; she didn't watch this injustice go down and drop to her knees to "pray about the situation." (There's a time to act and a time to pray.) Justice demanded that my daughter not hide behind fear with a spiritual veneer, and she behaved bravely.

That little girl spoke those words about Abby with as much reverence as a believer talking about God. And, in a sense, she saw a side of God. She saw someone fight for justice and defend the weak, someone dear to God's heart. My daughter reflected God's nature.

And what if Abby hadn't defended her? Perhaps either quickly or in time she might come to think that justice is a cheap trick, that cruelty rules. The truth is, like all evil, cruelty is ultimately a defeated foe; it only rules when the righteous fail to act.

DON'T FOCUS ON "FAIR"

Nice Guys believe that someday life will be fair if only they can discover some secret formula to avoiding difficulty. It's as if they want a break from all the hardships that have befallen them. While this is in some ways understandable, it's also false and dangerous wishful thinking.

Life *is* difficult, as Jesus promised; the sooner we embrace this, the better, and not teaching it to our children is a form of abuse. When my son tells me he's scared at nighttime, I sometimes say, "Pal, just remember, when this world scares you, there's a lot to be scared about." It's a joke and we both laugh, but it's a joke with a purpose—I want him to know this world brings serious challenges that are difficult to surmount. The challenges *aren't* insurmountable; I only want him to accept that they're going to be present, and I don't want him to be shocked when life is unfair.

Everyone has licked wounds. CNGs, though, lick wounds until they become worse wounds. Unfairness becomes an obsession, so they kick at the darkness instead of seeking to allow daylight into their lives; all their misspent energy keeps them stuck. Heed the advice of Madame Jeanne Guyon:

> If knowing the answers to life's questions is absolutely necessary to you, then forget the journey. You will never make it, for this is a journey of unknowables . . . and most of all, things unfair.

The more your life pulses with meaning and purpose, the more you'll find people wanting to stop you. Unfairness is the world's way—know this, and then don't let it stop you. Use Jesus as your model, because it never stopped him.

Do yourself a favor: Start charting a new life path through the unfairness. Instead of complaining about others, focus on you.

> **Life *is* difficult, as Jesus promised; the sooner we embrace this, the better, and not teaching it to our children is a form of abuse.**

Instead of praying to be delivered from life's inevitable difficulties, pray to be delivered from fear. Make yourself useful. If your career isn't working, acquire skills that businesses need, skills you could use to start your own enterprise if you choose. One practice that takes the sting out of workplace unfairness is making money outside of your paid job; this can help you feel more independent and confident, and it will also help you get out of your CNG foxhole.

CHOOSING TO BE PASSIVE

Though we've examined how assertiveness is normally our goal, there are times when choosing to be passive or aggressive is right. (Again, Jesus exemplified both—for instance, when he didn't answer questions and when he picked up a whip.) *Acting out a form of passivity can be proactive when it's a conscious choice in a given situation.*

Koch and Haugk point out the following in *Speaking the Truth in Love: How to Be an Assertive Christian:*

> When Lazarus was sick, Jesus delayed until Lazarus died. Jesus assertively chose not to resist when he was betrayed, arrested in the garden, put on trial, and mocked by his captors. And, in an intriguing story in Matthew 17:24–27, Jesus assertively chose not to give offense and instead to pay the unfair and arbitrary temple tax.

They list other meaningful examples of choosing passivity:

o Consider passivity when someone is already apologizing. It does neither you nor him any good to assert yourself. It's not gracious, and we likewise don't want people to hand us our head when we acknowledge our wrongdoing.

o Consider passivity when being assertive could seriously hurt another. When you know that someone is going through a life crisis and he speaks to you in such a way that he wouldn't otherwise, it's kind to let it pass. Perhaps discuss it at a different time, or let it go completely. If that dark cloud passes and the behavior continues, it's another matter.

o Consider passivity if being assertive puts your life or the lives of others in danger. For example, if you're being robbed at gunpoint, better to temporarily relinquish your rights than run the risk of being shot.

o Consider passivity when assertiveness is likely to cause imminent personal loss. If you think what you may say or do may lose you your job and you need it, consider waiting till you have another job opportunity. It may make sense to be passive at work but assertive behind the scenes.

One final piece of practical advice: When becoming a Christian Good Guy, you will make mistakes. But here's the great news: God doesn't expect you to be perfect, and neither do normal people.

When you make an error, apologize with sincerity and without groveling. Healthy people don't expect you to grovel; ill people do. You aren't even responsible for whether or not someone accepts your apology; you are only responsible to own up to your actions. Walk away from someone who says otherwise.

In fact, avoid even trying to figure out why he has this expectation. If someone requires perfection from you, that's his problem. Hopefully you don't expect perfection from others, so why would you think *you* have to do it right all the time?

Healthy people don't expect you to grovel; ill people do. You aren't even responsible for whether or not someone accepts your apology; you are only responsible to own up to your actions. Walk away from someone who says otherwise.

I have a team of men I call and meet with while on this Christian Good Guy journey. They share in my victories and help me not to overreact to my defeats. No one gets it right all the time. This road isn't easy to stay on, but it's much easier than the CNG's zigzag life.

This better life is made easier when you have people encouraging you. Mark Twain said he could live for weeks off of one sincere compliment. You'll need compliments and other encouragement from a trusted band of brothers and sisters, the kind of group Christ created around himself and encouraged his disciples to create when he sent them out in tandem. If you find you don't need this support, then you aren't yet on the Christian Good Guy Highway.

CHAPTER

GOD: LION OR COCKER SPANIEL?

A good battle plan that you act on today can be better than a perfect one tomorrow.
— GEORGE S. PATTON

We know what we are, but know not what we may be.
— WILLIAM SHAKESPEARE

I used to wonder if our reluctance to embrace Jesus' bold manner is an attempt to remake God into a safe Supreme Nice Guy. I no longer wonder. We ignore his assertive and sometimes tough manner because we want to declaw the Lion of Judah. We want the Lion to be a happy cocker spaniel, the animal kingdom's equivalent of a Nice Guy.

God—Father, Son, and Holy Spirit—has undergone an ill-advised cultural surgery, an operation we think will make our lives safer, when it really makes them more dangerous; we usually don't see the damage this does until it's too late. Getting us to believe that niceness and goodness are synonymous is one of evil's most successful ploys in our time.

There is a rabbinical legend that captures a conversation between angels and God. The angels ask, "Tell us about this messiah figure. Why is he so special? What will make him distinct?"

God replies, "Messiah is one who will stand straight."

The historical record shows that Jesus stood far straighter than we currently acknowledge. By bending him to our preference, we make it harder for both Jews and Gentiles to recognize and follow him. Dr. M. Scott Peck saw this fact when he hosted international workshops. People from many different religions attended, and he observed that each group consistently demonstrated certain traits. For example, Jews were often challenging. Muslims, didactic. Christians? "Nice. And it especially bothered Muslims," he says. Islamists saw that Christians weren't being honest about what they really believed and how they really lived. By implication they represented a weak faith.

Still, we humans just can't seem to help ourselves. We want the world to be a nice and undemanding place, even when God said it never has been and never will be. Something in us desires a comfortable God, a comfortable faith, a comfortable life, so we're reluctant to butt heads with a culture that wants to destroy masculinity or with a church that continues the Effeminate Jesus myth. Numbing niceness still pumps like ether through sanctuary air ducts on any given Sunday. Many frustrated men gasp for pure air, many exasperated women are lonely, and many children feel abandoned and nervous. The world sees more and more corruption because a critical redemptive power is not widely activated; the potential for heroism could be lost on yet another generation.

> **Getting us to believe that niceness and goodness are synonymous is one of evil's most successful ploys in our time.**

There's a maxim in the world of outdoor activity: Cotton kills—it keeps you warm until it gets wet. Rely on something else, something less comfortable but more reliable, like wool, if you want to stay alive. We should have a similar principle when it comes to spiritual growth: Comfort kills. This doesn't mean we should shun all comfort, that we shouldn't take shelter from time to time from life's hardships. Nevertheless, we should recognize that comfort encumbers us, and it nails Christian Nice Guys with a kind of death by a thousand stabbings. Remember, CNGs believe they have no real choices, so they stay in comfortable but abusive jobs, tolerate comfortable but void-of-respect relationships, and continue to attend comfortable churches that make them feel ashamed for being human. (While none of those things is truly comfortable, the CNG often thinks that *anything* is more comfortable than conflict and change.)

ENLIST OR DODGE

> **Don't allow deceptive fear or expedient theology to stop you from strapping on a pair of boots.**

This book is an invitation to join the Good Guy Rebellion, and if you've come this far, then it's more than an invitation: It's a draft notice, and you have a choice to enlist or flee. Fear keeps you from engaging, from being like Christ, as does a theology that says, "The destruction I see all around me—it's all predestined, part of the world's last days." No such weak excuse ever came from the lips of our faith's early heroes. Many stood, fought, and delivered without any assurance of victory; they exercised faith in the face of amazing opposition. God is an odds-breaker—he loves that game, and when you flex even a small amount of faith, he'll open doors for you. Don't allow deceptive fear or expedient theology to stop you from strapping on a pair of boots.

THE EXISTENCE OF EVIL

In order for the remedies to CNG passivity to be effective, you must also wrestle with the following question: Is there evil in this world, and, if so, how does it impact my life? Many Christians don't live as if there is, and many don't think there's a destroyer of their souls, though Jesus said to pray for deliverance from that destroyer. The destroyer wants you to stay in numb comfort, unwilling to awaken and address the difficult reality. He doesn't want you to realize what C. S. Lewis wrote: "The safest road to hell is the gradual one—the gentle slope, soft underfoot, without sudden turnings, without milestones, without signposts" (*The Screwtape Letters*). Sound like the life you've been living? You've worked so hard for a smooth ride, but now you've realized it really isn't smooth. The day you admit this is a day of victory.

Evil doesn't want you to enlist in the Good Guy Rebellion. It wants you to think that even if you know comfort's killing you, there's no other road to turn onto. That's a lie as well. I wrote this book to show you there *is* a way out. God in his mercy has not left you to wander another day in Niceland; you'll have to make the decision of whether or not to follow the other way.

Dr. Laura says that "being nice in the face of evil makes you a victim," and this is the same evil that keeps you in passivity. May this fact keep you awake tonight, because, despite our inclinations, such disquietude is good for us. I thank God for my nocturnal wrestling from a place of soul-trouble; that's one of his ways of telling us there's something truly wrong inside.

Starting to see God for who he really is changes the way we approach him and the way we live. We are more secure and loved, not less, which produces the boldness and honesty we need for meaningful lives. Writes P. T. Forsyth:

> Cast yourself into his arms, not to be caressed, but to wrestle with him. He loves that holy war. He may . . . lift you from your feet. But it will be to lift you from the earth, and set you in the heavenly places which are theirs who fight the good fight and lay hold of God as their eternal life. (*The Soul of Prayer*)

We should be thankful we don't serve a nice God, because such an entity would have no real power to help us. Annie Dillard writes regarding God's true nature,

> Does anyone have the foggiest idea of what sort of power we so blithely invoke? The churches are children playing on the floor with their chemistry sets, mixing up a batch of TNT to kill a Sunday morning. It's madness to wear ladies' straw hats and velvet hats to church; we should all be wearing crash helmets. (*Travelers Unaware*)

I found Crash-Helmet Jesus by stumbling upon him when I wasn't looking for him. I didn't want this Jesus; he scared me. That makes me smile today, because I know it wasn't some wish fulfillment, a Freudian term used by critics of God to dismiss spiritual conviction. The real Jesus wasn't a cultural icon or an image of my making. Few wish for a tougher Jesus, one who makes us face our fears—until they see how it sets them free from the shackles of passivity and all the misery therein.

THE CHRISTIAN GOOD GUY LIFE

I'm often asked by men and women what this transformed life will look like. Here's a sneak preview of what you can expect.

You'll find that you actually enjoy a good challenge. You'll be like the guys who saw an advertisement from Ernest Shackleton seeking help with his exploration of the South Pole in the early 1900s: "Men wanted for hazardous journey; small wages, bitter cold, long months of complete darkness, constant danger, safe return doubtful, honor and recognition in case of success." More than five thousand men, from suntanned sailors to Cambridge-educated scientists, answered the advertisement. Many were surely tired of dullness and comfort in the lives they'd created for themselves. Those who joined the expedition found adventure and, in the process, made history.

Your life will still have patches of rough travel, but it won't feel as tough. You'll have less grit in your mental gears. Your part in this grand play of life will be more passionate. Healthy people will love and appreciate the changes in you.

You'll make sacrifices to obtain abundant life and embark on new paths. Sometimes this will mean stripping life of certain comforts in order to flourish—inside a guy's heart there's meant to be a respect for lean living, as described in Paul's first letter to the younger Timothy (6:9–11). If simpler living doesn't invigorate your masculine sensibility, then it's probably dormant or neglected; you may need to scale back on material possessions for a while. Offloading your "stuff" can be like using smelling salts, and this kind of clearing your head helps you to discern God's will.

You will challenge the commonly accepted order. Like Christ, you will no longer be able to accept the world as it is. You will stand up for those in need and thereby fulfill the command of God through the prophet Isaiah. You will seek justice, encourage the oppressed, defend the fatherless, and plead the case of widows. You will at times be unable to remain silent. Writes Rick Bundschuh: "An energy that breaks the status quo should be expected when the spirit of the One who overturned tables pulses through the veins of men who serve him" (*Passed Thru Fire*).

You will encourage your kids to help others, like my friend Bill who was overweight as a boy; classmates picked on him for as long as he can remember. He's in his fifties now, still overweight, and when he tells me about the cruel words thrown at him during grade school, his eyes still water. The paint from that pain just won't dry.

You will stand up for those in need. You will seek justice, encourage the oppressed, defend the fatherless, and plead the case of widows. You will at times be unable to remain silent.

I have said on my talk show that during the live broadcast some kid in our community will be picked on because of his weight. And a child who attended Sunday school that week will witness the cruelty. And it will be rare, if at all, that even one shows the courage, bravery, or integrity to stand up for the fat kid.

Why? Because popular Christianity does not encourage or even accept that response—kids are encouraged to be nice, sweet, gentle doves instead. *We are encouraged to be bold only when it comes to being evangelical. Or giving money.* You, a warrior of light, will push against our abominable record with injustice by creating smaller warriors of light. God will be pleased.

I made breakfast recently for my daughter and her eight-year-old friend who had spent the night. The friend's mother is dying of cancer.

No one can say how long she has to live. Oncologists washed their hands, said their parting words, and moved on to other patients months ago. All I really know is that there's this little bright-eyed girl in my kitchen who's consuming my buttermilk waffles, and she's grateful. "I come from a waffle family," she tells me with a perfect smile.

She's witty and well-adjusted, adept at keen observations. What matters to her this icy Sunday morning is that I get out of the way so she can watch Allison Krause's slow-motion, melancholy music video on our kitchen television. Her mind isn't on what I'm thinking about: How much of her mother was claimed by cancer last night, no more than a mile away.

It's hard to look at her sweet face. I'm tempted to give in to Snivels, the inner coward, and hide behind my busyness, for I know what's coming. During the routine of life, between going to work, taking out the garbage, and paying bills, we'll eventually get a call as cold and dark as lead, telling us what's both expected and shocking. A husband will lose his wife, four children their mother.

We the living will be called into action, a band of relievers summoned from the bullpen. We will help her family bear its grief and whatever other emotions flow. But now, because Nice Guy passivity doesn't control me— I'm no longer such a weenie—I'm up to the task. I won't, as in years past, hide outside the funeral home with all the smokers (I don't even smoke). I won't survey horizons that can't console, stare at mute oak trees that give no answers. I'll be in there—with one shell of a woman, many who loved her, soft lights, tender music, and warm biblical assurances—where the redemptive work is done.

I'll weep with those who weep. I'll console. I won't try to fix. True, in there will be the epicenter of something I won't understand. Who really understands death? But because courage and faith flow where once they could not, I won't run. I will do what I can to suck the venom from this world's cursed snakebites.

Sometimes when I think about my boyhood—when the Nice Guy problem began for me—I entertain the thought of traveling back in time to give myself a pep talk. I want to talk sense to that scared and conflicted boy, the one who mumbled around adults and frequently flinched because he believed even strangers had the right and the will to hit him—all the nervous habits that accompany physical abuse. I want to coax life out from within him, life that was smothered under doubt, self-loathing, and rage— all those feelings that go along with emotional abuse and neglect. I want him to come alive against the odds, to show uncommon valor, bravery rarely seen in men—the kind that the Irish appreciate, that Hollywood exploits, and that portions of the Bible celebrate.

Someone *did* have this kind of conversation with me once. A man who appeared to be in his thirties consoled me. He was a stranger, and he came out of nowhere, though not in a startling or theatrical way. He was wearing a long-sleeved plaid shirt and had longer, light brown hair. This was the '70s after all—he was dressed for the times.

I was especially troubled that sunny but chilly morning in Reseda, California, so, like usual, I went outside. I needed to be outside. And there he found me. I don't remember the exact words of his counsel. But I felt loved afterward. And free. It was a newly minted feeling for me: lofree.

This stranger didn't come to talk with me; he came to announce. He looked like he was in a hurry, even though he didn't speak fast. He spoke as someone who possessed important information, the way messengers speak in war movies, except he wasn't nervous.

He knew my soul, and he reinforced it not so much with happiness but with resolve. I glimpsed that I wouldn't always be so small and frightened, or this world so large and beguiling. Hope flowed through the dry cracks within me.

Then suddenly he was gone, his exit as unexpected as his appearance. I looked around for him, a life preserver thrown to me in roiling waters. I wanted more of this feeling that was both dreamy and practical.

He left me with a bedrock blessing, not a Nice Guy grin or a long-winded prayer. He didn't try to put a happy face on things either—he was good, and he was shrewd, and he wouldn't have settled for weak pleasantries. Somehow he knew my painful circumstances, so he imparted soul food, not sugary candy, for the waves of abuse still to come.

He didn't slap me on the back and say, "Count it all joy, brother," which a Christian Nice Guy did only days after my mother died in dire and depressing conditions. *This* moment was medicinal, visceral—it couldn't have been kept shallow with good vibrations that would have had no power to fortify a soul like mine.

I call that stranger Major Good Guy, the Anti-Nice Guy. Was he an angel? I still wonder. I would not meet another with that kind of restoring power until I met the real tough-to-tender Jesus.

What *would* have happened if I had managed to travel back in time and ferret out that little boy during my fantasy conversation? Honestly, I have to admit I would have coaxed him to bloom in a place that was unintentionally hostile toward such growth. It's best to guard your heart in such situations when you have no choice of setting. There's a time to hide just as there's a time to stand and deliver.

> **You have the choice to become extraordinary. You choose a half life if you don't; Jesus did *not* live and die to set only half of you free.**

You and I have a choice today to stand and deliver. Don't ever let yourself grow tired of hearing and applying this—it's the chemotherapy to your cancer. You can unchain your heart and renew your mind, to help both to grow as never before. By God's grace you can come alive, and you can experience the adventurous joy of seeing the world around you redeemed. Good *can* come from bad—that's no fairy tale.

George Orwell's observation that ordinary men are passive is as factual as gravity—the mass of men lie down and let life happen to them. But you aren't called to be ordinary. You have the choice to become extraordinary. You choose a half life if you don't; Jesus did *not* live and die to set only half of you free.

Grow boldly, brothers. And, as you help them, sisters, know that your love is a reality that cannot be dismantled. *Love endures all things.*